"I THOUGHT I WAS JUST WEIRD": THRIVING AFTER A LATE ADHD & AUTISM DIAGNOSIS

A Candid, Culture-Savvy Guide for Women & BIPOC Navigating Neurodivergent Adulthood

Nicci Brochard

&

Dr. Ben Chuba

For permissions, licensing, or inquiries, please contact

info@crossborderpublishers.com
www.crossborderpublishers.com

Book Formatting by: *Monish*

Book cover design by: *FaTima*

New York, London, Quebec

Contents

Foreword

For most of my life, I thought something was *off* but not in a way I could explain. I was always "too much" of something: too sensitive, too forgetful, too intense, too spacey, too blunt, too emotional, too distracted. People told me I was quirky, moody, or just plain difficult. At times, I believed them. I carried the quiet shame of being unable to keep up with "normal." I overcompensated, masked, burned out, and then did it all again. It wasn't until adulthood that I finally received the diagnosis that changed everything: ADHD *and* autism.

If you're reading this, you've been on a similar journey. Maybe you were recently diagnosed or are still figuring it out. Either way, welcome. This book is for you the late-diagnosed, the misdiagnosed, the misunderstood. Especially if you're a woman or a person of color, the path to understanding yourself through the lens of neurodivergence can be extra complicated. Cultural expectations, gender roles, and systemic bias often mean we're overlooked or dismissed entirely. The truth is many of us weren't *missed* we were *ignored.*

This is not a clinical textbook or a one-size-fits-all how-to guide. It's a candid, culturally aware, and real-world survival manual for navigating neurodivergent adulthood when you've spent a lifetime feeling like you were just "weird." We'll discuss masking, burnout, relationships, work, healing, unlearning shame, and reclaiming your identity. We'll also talk about what it means to thrive not by neurotypical standards but on your terms.

You don't need to be "fixed." You were never broken. You didn't have the whole picture, but now you do.

This book is your permission slip to rest, be messy, ask questions, and exist as your whole, unfiltered self. It's also a love letter to the inner child who was never given the language to say, *"I'm not weird I'm wired differently."*

Ben and I (Nicci) are excited to take this journey with you, and we promise you will find our research and guide helpful.

CHAPTER 1

The "Aha" Moment

A specific kind of relief and grief comes with finally knowing. For many of us, the moment we receive a diagnosis of ADHD or autism as adults feels like a lightbulb turning on in a room we didn't even realize was dark. Suddenly, so much of our past makes sense. The missed deadlines, the sensory overload, the social confusion, the burnout cycles, the deep need for routine none of it was because we were lazy, dramatic, or too sensitive. We were neurodivergent all along. We didn't have the words for it.

The "aha" moment can look different for everyone. Maybe it came after months of doom-scrolling through neurodivergent content and seeing yourself in every post. Perhaps it was sparked by a child's diagnosis or a mental health spiral that forced you to seek answers. Maybe someone you trust gently said, "Hey... have you ever looked into this?" However it happened, the realization hit hard: *I'm not broken. I'm just wired differently.*

This chapter is about honoring that moment; whether it was instant or came in slow waves. It's about exploring the emotional aftermath of finally having a name for your experiences. For women and BIPOC especially, that moment can feel both empowering and infuriating. Why didn't anyone notice sooner? Why did I have to figure this out myself?

The "aha" moment starts a journey, not the end. It's the first deep breath after years of holding it in. In this chapter, we'll unpack the power of that realization, the emotions that come with it, and how it sets the stage for healing, unlearning, and reclaiming your identity on your terms.

The Weird Little Clues You Missed (But Now Make Perfect Sense)

Before the diagnosis, life probably felt like an endless game of trying to "get it together" while watching everyone else make it look easy. You might've spent years blaming yourself for struggling with things that seemed effortless for others. You worked harder, stayed later, over-explained, over-apologized, and still felt like you were behind. But once the diagnosis clicked into place, a new realization emerged: *The clues were there all along.*

Looking back, the signs were subtle but loud in their way. Like puzzle pieces you never knew were missing, they now click together with surprising clarity. Let's talk about some weird little clues you probably brushed off, minimized, or chalked up to "just being weird."

1. You Were The "Sensitive One"

You cried easily. Loud noises or crowded spaces overwhelm you. Tags in your clothes made you squirm. People may have called you dramatic or emotional when experiencing the world with heightened sensitivity. Sensory processing differences are a common trait among both ADHD and autistic people but without the language to explain it, it just felt like a flaw. Now? It's a clue you were neurodivergent all along.

2. Your Brain Refused To Work On Command

Deadlines, tasks, and even basic chores often felt like impossible mountains. You wanted to do them you *planned* to do them, but your brain said, "Nope." Time got slippery. You either hyper focused for hours or couldn't start at all. You were told you were lazy, disorganized, or procrastinating on purpose. In reality, you were navigating executive dysfunction an invisible challenge that had nothing to do with your intelligence or effort.

3. Socializing Was A Mystery (And A Performance)

You either talked too much or not enough. Group dynamics were confusing. Small talk exhausted you. You rehearsed conversations ahead of time, replayed them afterward, and often felt like you were watching life happen from the outside. You may have learned how to "mask" early mirroring people, forcing eye contact, and pretending to be OK when you were not. At the time, it felt like survival. Now you realize it was also a clue.

Nicci Brochard & Dr. Ben Chuba

4. You Had Intense Interests (Aka Hyper fixations)

There were things you *loved* with your whole soul. Whether it was a TV show, a niche topic, or a hobby you dove into for hours without blinking, your passion burned bright. People might tease you for being "obsessed" or "doing the most." But for neurodivergent brains, those deep dives are joy, comfort, and even self-regulation. What once felt like "too much" now makes perfect sense.

5. Your Energy Came In Chaotic Waves

Some days, you were on fire creative, productive, unstoppable. On other days, getting out of bed felt impossible. You might've internalized this as laziness or inconsistency. But that boom-and-bust cycle is often the result of masking, burnout, sensory overload, or unrecognized needs. Your nervous system wasn't built for constant grind it needed rest, rhythm, and recovery.

6. You Never Really "Grew Out Of It"

Teachers said you were bright but "didn't apply yourself." The family called you spacey or emotional. As you got older, you tried harder to fit in. But the struggles didn't go away they just got quieter or better hidden. You may have spent your 20s or 30s thinking, *Why is adulting so hard for me?* That lingering question was another clue: you weren't behind you were playing a whole different game with none of the right tools.

7. You Felt Like An Alien In Your Own Culture

Especially if you're BIPOC, the disconnect may have been even more profound. You were expected to behave a certain way, be strong, put together, and not complain. Neurodivergence isn't something many cultures openly talk about, and being "different" can feel dangerous. So you pushed your needs down, code-switched constantly, and perfected the art of performing normalcy. But all that effort? It was another giant clue: you weren't just "sensitive" or "awkward" you were surviving in a world that wasn't built for your brain.

The beauty of hindsight is that it offers clarity where confusion used to live. What once felt like random struggles now reveal themselves as patterns of a beautifully different brain doing its best without support. You weren't broken or weird. You were misunderstood.

Realizing this can come with a wave of emotions grief for the younger you who didn't have answers, anger at the systems that failed you, and relief in finally being seen. It's OK to sit with all of that. It's OK to mourn what could've been *if someone had noticed sooner.* And it's just OK to celebrate the fact that *you* saw it now.

This chapter invites you to revisit those past experiences with new eyes not to shame yourself for missing the signs, but to reclaim your story with compassion. Every "weird little clue" was a breadcrumb leading you back to yourself.

What Finally Pushed You To Seek A Diagnosis?

Getting a diagnosis in adulthood doesn't usually come from a neat, linear process. It's more like a series of quiet nudges, confusing patterns, and "wait a minute…" moments that build over time. For many of us, it wasn't about wanting a label it was about survival. Something inside said *This can't be normal. I shouldn't feel this exhausted from just existing.* So you started digging. You followed the signs. And eventually, you arrived at a truth you couldn't ignore: you weren't just quirky, lazy, dramatic, or disorganized. You were neurodivergent.

So what finally made it undeniable? Maybe it was burnout. Not the kind of burnout that resolves with a long weekend or a mental health day but the deep, soul-tired kind that comes from years of masking and pushing yourself to meet invisible standards. You felt like you were doing everything "right" working hard, people-pleasing, trying to stay on top of your life but still falling apart. The emotional labor, the sensory overload, and the constant internal pressure it all added up until your system crashed.

Or it was motherhood. Or auntie-hood. Or becoming a mentor. Watching a child struggle with focus, emotional regulation, or social connection might've felt eerily familiar. You saw pieces of yourself in them. You started reading articles, listening to podcasts, diving into late-night rabbit holes and the more you learned about ADHD or autism, the more you saw your reflection staring back. It wasn't just about the child anymore. It became personal.

For others, the turning point was therapy. Maybe you'd been in and out of counseling for years, always feeling like something was missing. Depression, anxiety, trauma sure, those labels felt partly true. But they didn't fully explain the disconnect you thought from the world around you. Eventually, a therapist said the quiet part out loud: "Have you ever considered ADHD? Or autism?" And suddenly, everything stopped. *Wait what? Me?* The suggestion felt both strange and strangely right.

Sometimes, it wasn't a professional at all. It was TikTok. Or Instagram. Or Reddit. You stumbled across a video or a post with a caption like, "Signs you might have ADHD as an adult" or "Autistic traits you didn't know were autistic." At first, it was a curiosity click. Then, it was ten more videos. Then a playlist. Then, a deep breath as you whispered to yourself, "Is this… me?" It was like someone spied on your entire life and turned it content. And for once, it made sense.

It could have come from a friend someone who recognized the patterns or who had recently been diagnosed themselves. They shared their story, and it unlocked something inside you. You saw yourself in their experiences not just the struggles but the *why* behind them. That "me too" moment was powerful. It cracked open the possibility that you didn't imagine your difficulty navigating the world that your suffering had context.

Maybe it was the pandemic. When the usual routines disappeared, so did the systems that helped you cope? Suddenly, you were working from home, overwhelmed by the unstructured time. Or isolation gave you the stillness to reflect. All the noise and distraction fell away, and what was left? A brain that couldn't rest, a body that couldn't regulate, and a mind racing to keep up with itself. You realized your coping skills weren't just quirks they were lifelines. Without them, everything unraveled.

For BIPOC adults, especially women, the road to diagnosis is often extra-long and winding. Cultural expectations, survival instincts, and systemic barriers usually delay the realization. We're taught to be strong, push through, and not make a scene. If you were told to pray about it, tough it out, or stop being dramatic, then, of course, you internalized the idea that your struggles were personal weaknesses not signs of a deeper neurodivergence. It can take years, even decades, to unlearn that narrative.

And yet, here you are. Something pushed you to ask: *What if it's not just me finally?* That question might've come with fear, shame, or even disbelief. But it also came with hope. The hope that maybe just maybe there was a way to live with more ease, clarity, and self-compassion.

Seeking a diagnosis as an adult is brave, vulnerable, and profoundly validating. Once you know the truth, you can stop performing and start healing. You can stop chasing an impossible version of "normal" and begin designing a life that honors your needs.

What pushed you to seek a diagnosis might have been dramatic, or it might have been quiet. It might've looked like a meltdown or sitting silently in your car, not knowing how to proceed. It might've come after years of therapy or one compelling meme. Whatever the path it matters. It brought you here.

And now that you know, you can never un-know. That's the beauty and the burden of the "aha" moment. But it's also the beginning of something new. Not easy. Not magical. But real. And real is powerful.

Breaking Through The Myths: "But You're Doing Fine!" And Other Lies

One of the most common and most damaging responses to a late ADHD or autism diagnosis is, *"But you're doing fine!"* It's often said with good intentions but lands like a slap. It's a dismissal wrapped in a compliment. As if the years you spent barely holding it together were proof that you didn't need help. It is as if appearing functional means you were never struggling in the first place.

But here's the truth: masking is not thriving. Survival is not the same as wellness. And high-functioning is a myth built on the erasure of invisible labor.

You might've looked like you had it all under control from the outside. You went to school. You got the degree. You held down a job. You smiled at the correct times, laughed at the right jokes, showed up to the events, and maybe even earned a few gold stars along the way. But people didn't see the behind-the-scenes chaos the mental gymnastics, the emotional exhaustion, the burnout that hit like a freight train the minute you got home. You were "doing fine" by other people's standards. But no one saw the cost.

No one saw how long it took to prepare for social interactions. It was hard to focus through meetings or conversations while your brain sprinted in ten directions. How emotionally flooded you feel after small talk, noise, or bright lights. You had to script and rehearse fundamental interactions to avoid saying the "wrong thing." You punished yourself for being "too much" or "not enough."

The myth of "you're doing fine" also shows up in other forms:

- "You're too smart to have ADHD."

- "You're too social to be autistic."

- "You made it this far; what's the problem now?"

- "You don't *look* like someone with... (insert diagnosis)."

These comments aren't just annoying they're harmful. They're rooted in stereotypes, shaped by outdated diagnostic models built around white, cisgender boys. For women and BIPOC, especially, these myths have kept us undiagnosed, unsupported, and silently suffering for decades. We became experts in adapting. Experts in pushing through. And the world rewarded our suffering by calling it "success."

But that success came at a cost: anxiety, depression, chronic burnout, self-doubt, and, in many cases, health issues that stemmed from years of ignoring our needs. When someone tells you "you were doing fine," they only look at the mask, not the person behind it.

It's time to rewrite the narrative. You were never "fine." You were doing the best you could with no answers, no language, and no support. That's not nothing, that's resilience. But resilience shouldn't be required to get through daily life.

You deserved to be supported, not just praised for coping quietly. You deserved accommodations, not applause for overextending. You deserved understanding, not confusion when you couldn't follow the "simple" instructions everyone else seemed to grasp.

The myth of "fine" is one of the most significant barriers to late diagnosis. It makes us doubt ourselves, feel like imposters, and think maybe we're just making excuses. But deep down, you know the truth. You always knew something was different.

Breaking through these myths means finally naming what's real. It means letting go of the idea that your struggles weren't valid just because you managed to function. It means honoring the effort it took to appear OK when you barely held it together.

Getting diagnosed doesn't erase the past, but it helps you see it through a new lens a more compassionate one. One that says, *"You weren't crazy. You weren't lazy. You were neurodivergent in a world that didn't see you."*

And now? Now you see yourself. That changes everything.

Chapter 2

Diagnosis In Adulthood: Relief, Rage, And Realness

Getting diagnosed with ADHD or autism as an adult is not just a moment it's a *collision*. It's the crashing together of past, present, and future. Everything shifts when someone says the words, confirms your suspicions, or hands over the official paperwork. You finally have a name for the thing that's shaped your whole life. And while that can bring a wave of *relief*, it often arrives hand-in-hand with *rage* and a heavy dose of *realness*.

For many of us, a late diagnosis is both validation and grief. Validation because we always *knew* something was different. We couldn't explain it, and no one around us could. We were misread, mislabeled, or missed altogether especially if we were women, BIPOC, or grew up in communities where mental health wasn't talked about, let alone neurodivergence.

And then there's the rage, rage for the years spent confused and self-critical, for the punishments we endured, the friendships that fell apart, the opportunities that slipped through our fingers not because we weren't capable, but because we didn't have the language or support. It's the fury of realizing you were expected to succeed in a system never designed with you in mind.

But once the diagnosis settles in, a different kind of realness emerges: a clearer picture of your past, a new understanding of your patterns, and, eventually, a profound, often emotional reckoning with who you are *without the mask*. The diagnosis doesn't fix everything, but it opens a door. It permits you to stop pretending, to start asking for what you need, and to live, maybe for the first time, in alignment with how your brain works.

This chapter explores the layered emotions that come with a late diagnosis: the joy, the grief, the anger, the clarity, and the radical self-compassion that starts to grow when you finally hear the words: *You're not broken. You're neurodivergent.*

Emotional Whiplash: Validation, Grief, And Anger

Receiving a late diagnosis of ADHD or autism doesn't just come with a wave of relief it comes with a rollercoaster of emotions that can feel like *whiplash*. The mix of validation, grief, and anger can be overwhelming. After years of struggling without answers, the sudden clarity brings intense emotional reactions that are often complex and conflicting. Here's a breakdown of the three key emotions that many people experience after a late diagnosis:

1. Validation: The Weight Of The Truth

Validation is one of the first emotions you feel, often the one that feels the most immediate. Finally, you have a word to describe the disjointed pieces of your life the constant feeling that something was "off," but you could never put your finger on it. The diagnosis feels like a key that opens a locked door. The experiences that you've had, the struggles you've faced, suddenly make sense.

You may feel an overwhelming sense of *yes; that's me* when you first learn about ADHD or autism. The long history of missed social cues, the chronic disorganization, the overstimulation that left you drained suddenly, these aren't quirks or personality flaws. They are part of a real neurological difference. That feeling of relief can be liberating, like breathing for the first time in a room in which you've spent your whole life trapped.

At last, the things you've struggled with are no longer "failures." They are symptoms. Symptoms of something you couldn't control, but something that now has a name. And in that moment, you realize that you weren't crazy, lazy, or broken after all.

2. Grief: The Loss Of A "Normal" Life

But along with that validation comes a deep sense of grief. This emotion often hits hardest the realization that so much of your life has been shaped by a lack of understanding, and the weight of all that lost time begins to sink in. You've been trying to fit into a world that wasn't designed for you for years. You've probably suffered silently, pushing yourself harder than most, only to fail repeatedly in ways that felt personal.

The grief isn't just for the lost time it's for the relationships that may have been affected by your neurodivergence, for the missed opportunities, and for the parts of your life you spent pretending to be someone you're not. It's about all the times you hid your struggles, masked your true self, or tried to "force" yourself to meet expectations that never aligned with your brain's natural rhythms. There's a pain in knowing that you've spent years not knowing what you needed, or worse, not even realizing that you *needed* anything different.

This grief can manifest as sadness for your past self. The child was told to "try harder" when she was already trying as hard as possible. The teenager who felt "weird" didn't have the language to express why. The adult who struggled in silence, believing she was just "too much" or "not enough."

3. Anger: The Burden Of Being Misunderstood

Alongside validation and grief comes anger. Anger at the world for not seeing you and for not offering the support you needed. Anger at the systems that overlooked your struggles and at the people who brushed off your challenges as "quirks" or "excuses." Anger at the years of feeling like you weren't *enough*, not because you weren't, but because the world did not understand how your brain worked.

For many women and BIPOC individuals, this anger is compounded by the societal and cultural pressure to be strong, resilient, and "normal." We are often expected to excel without accommodation or understanding. When we don't, we are labeled lazy, dramatic, or "too emotional." You might find yourself thinking: *Why didn't someone notice sooner? Why did I have to fight so hard to get this diagnosis?* The anger that comes with this realization is justified. It's a natural response to feeling unseen, unheard, and unsupported for so long.

This anger can also be directed inward. You may wonder how you missed the signs. Why didn't you recognize your own needs earlier? Self-blame can be intense, but it's important to remind yourself that you did the best you could with the information you had at the time. In a world that doesn't prioritize neurodivergence, it's not your fault that the signs went unnoticed.

4. The Emotional Whiplash

What makes the experience so disorienting is the emotional whiplash that comes with these conflicting feelings. One minute, you're feeling empowered by the validation of finally having a name for your experiences, and the next minute, you're overwhelmed by sadness or frustration at how long it took to get here. The rapid switching between relief, grief, and anger can feel like you're being pulled in multiple directions with no clear emotional anchor.

In many ways, your emotional experience mirrors the journey of accepting yourself as neurodivergent: messy, unstructured, and full of emotional highs and lows. But over time, this emotional whiplash can start to level out. You begin to make peace with the diagnosis, not as a final answer, but as a starting point a way to understand yourself in a world that often feels ill-equipped to understand neurodivergent minds.

5. The Path Forward

Eventually, the emotional rollercoaster slows down. Once you've processed the initial wave of validation, grief, and anger, you begin to move forward with a new sense of clarity. You start to build a life that considers your needs not as a crutch but as a foundation for growth. It's about learning to care for yourself, ask for help, and advocate for the accommodations you deserve.

But that journey doesn't erase the emotions you've felt. The validation, grief, and anger all remain part of your story, woven into the fabric of who you are. But you no longer have to live in them. You can live alongside them, knowing that with the diagnosis comes the power to reframe your past and reshape your future.

Why Bipoc & Women Are Often Missed

If you're a woman or a person of color or both it's not surprising that your ADHD or autism diagnosis came late. It's incredibly common. You weren't missed because the signs weren't there. You were missed because the system was never built to see *you* in the first place.

There's a long, painful history of medical, psychological, and educational systems being shaped around a very narrow idea of what ADHD and autism look like. For decades, the "standard" model has been based on white, cisgender boys kids who were hyperactive, disruptive, and visibly "off track" in classroom settings. If that wasn't you, the assumption was that you were fine. So what happens to everyone else?

1. The Science Wasn't Made With Us In Mind

Most of the early research on neurodivergence focused almost exclusively on young white boys. Their behaviors restlessness, impulsivity, meltdowns became the blueprint for diagnosis. However, ADHD and autism can present very differently in girls and BIPOC children. Instead of acting out, many of us learned to internalize. We shut down, stayed quiet, fawned to avoid conflict, and overcorrected ourselves constantly. While some boys were getting support plans and therapy referrals, we were told to stop daydreaming, try harder, or behave ourselves.

Even today, the diagnostic tools and screening checklists used by professionals are often based on outdated, gendered, and racially biased criteria. That means women and BIPOC are still far more likely to be overlooked, misdiagnosed with anxiety or depression, or dismissed altogether.

2. Cultural Expectations And Code-Switching

In many cultures especially within Black, Latinx, Asian, and Indigenous communities there's enormous pressure to conform, succeed, and keep your struggles private. We're often taught that showing emotion or asking for help is a weakness. Neurodivergence is rarely named or understood; instead, it's usually seen as "acting out," being "weird," or not being disciplined enough.

For girls and women, the pressure is compounded. We're expected to be polite, agreeable, helpful, and emotionally intuitive. So what do many of us do? We learn to mask. We become chameleons. We perform the version of ourselves that others want to see, and we do it so well that even our closest friends and family don't know we're struggling.

This kind of long-term masking takes a massive emotional toll and disconnects us from ourselves. Because we're working so hard to appear functional, people assume we don't need help. But just because someone *looks* OK doesn't mean they *are* OK.

3. Bias In The Medical And Educational Systems

Let's be real: systemic bias in healthcare and education is still a considerable barrier. Studies show that BIPOC children are less likely to be referred for evaluations and more likely to be disciplined or criminalized for behaviors that would be medicalized in white children. A Black girl zoning out in class might be labeled "defiant." A Latina girl struggling with organization might be told she's lazy. An Asian student may be assumed to be "too smart" to have ADHD. These stereotypes run deep, and they have long-term consequences.

Even when BIPOC individuals *do* seek help, they're often dismissed or misdiagnosed. Women are frequently told their symptoms are hormonal, stress-related, or just signs of anxiety. Men of color are often pathologized instead of supported. Many of our communities have a deep mistrust toward these systems, and that mistrust is earned. It makes seeking a diagnosis or treatment feel risky or even dangerous.

4. We Learned To Excel In Survival Mode

Because we had to, many of us became experts in overcompensation. We were the ones who got straight As but cried every night from being overwhelmed. We were the ones who held everything together for our families while silently falling apart. We worked twice as hard to be taken half as seriously. And when we did succeed, people assumed we were fine.

But that "success" came at a cost. We sacrificed sleep, health, boundaries, and self-worth to keep up. Our nervous systems were constantly in fight-or-flight. The breakdowns, meltdowns, and identity crises happened behind closed doors. By the time we were finally diagnosed often in our 20s, 30s, or 40s we were emotionally exhausted and profoundly disconnected from who we were.

5. The Myth Of The "Perfect Victim"

There's a silent stereotype that only certain kinds of people "deserve" diagnosis or support. You're supposed to look disheveled but not too messy, struggling but still functioning, expressive but not angry, vulnerable but not dramatic. When you don't fit the mold or when you challenge it you get overlooked.

For BIPOC women especially, there's often no room to be messy, weird, or different. We're expected to be caretakers, hustlers, and fixers. There's no space to say, *"Hey, my brain works differently, and I need support."* We're told to be strong, but strong doesn't mean we don't need understanding.

If you've ever asked yourself, *Why didn't anyone notice sooner?* The answer is: it's not your fault. You were missed because the system wasn't built with you in mind. You were surviving in a world that couldn't or wouldn't see your full humanity. But that doesn't make your experience any less valid.

Now, you get to write a new story where your needs matter. Where your neurodivergence is recognized, respected, and even celebrated, it's OK to grieve the time you lost. But it's also OK to feel proud of how far you've come despite everything working against you.

How The System Failed Us And How We Rise Anyway

Let's be clear: the system failed us. Not just once but repeatedly. It failed us in the classroom, where our struggles were overlooked, misunderstood, or punished. It failed us in healthcare settings, where we were misdiagnosed, dismissed, or ignored. It failed us in our families and communities, where cultural stigmas around mental health and neurodivergence made it nearly impossible even to *name* what we were going through.

For those of us who are women and/or BIPOC, the failure cuts even deeper. We were never the default. We weren't in the textbooks. We weren't in the training videos. Our pain didn't look like the kind they were taught to recognize. And so, instead of being supported, we learned to perform. To mask. To push through. To survive in silence.

We were told we were just lazy, emotional, or complex. We were told to toughen up, calm down, and try harder. We internalized those messages, and they shaped how we saw ourselves over time. Instead of asking, *"What support do I need?"* we asked, *"What's wrong with me?"* That question haunted us for years.

1. A System Built For Someone Else

The systems we interact with education, healthcare, employment were not designed with neurodivergent people in mind, especially not those of us outside the white, male, middle-class default. In school, students who couldn't sit still, daydreamed, or needed more time to process were labeled problems, not potential. In the workplace, the expectation to perform in rigid, overstimulating environments with constant deadlines often led to burnout not because we weren't capable, but because the structure was never flexible enough to support us.

Even when we sought help, we often hit brick walls: long waitlists, gatekeeping professionals, outdated assessment tools that didn't reflect our lived experience, and therapists and doctors who didn't listen or didn't believe us.

And yet, we're still here.

2. Rising Anyway

We rose not because the system got better but because *we* got louder. We started asking questions, finding each other, and sharing stories. We began unlearning the lies we were told about our worth and our ability. We finally stopped asking for permission to understand ourselves.

- We rise when we name our neurodivergence without shame.
- We rise when we advocate for accommodations and refuse to apologize for needing them.
- We rise by creating our communities, spaces, and tools that reflect *our* experiences.

Rising doesn't always look like a significant, dramatic change. Sometimes, it seems like permitting yourself to rest, saying no to things that drain you, and letting go of the pressure to perform. It looks like recognizing that "high functioning" is just code for "suffering quietly" and choosing not to wear that label like a badge anymore.

3. Healing Is Revolutionary

Every time you choose self-compassion over self-criticism, that's a revolution. You're breaking a cycle every time you give yourself what you needed as a child structure, softness, and space to be fully yourself. You are healing in a world that never made space for your kind of brain. That's not just brave. It's powerful.

We rise by reconnecting to our bodies, intuition, and joy. We rise by making peace with our past, not by pretending it didn't hurt but by acknowledging it and still choosing to move forward. We rise by telling the truth, our truth loudly, quietly, fiercely, and tenderly. However, it needs to come out.

We also rise by helping each other, by naming what we were never taught to name, by showing up for other neurodivergent folks, especially the ones still figuring it out and by holding space for those who've been silenced or sidelined. Because community is how we thrive, we were never meant to do this alone.

4. The System May Be Broken, But We Are Not

It's OK to be angry, and it's OK to grieve. The systems that failed us did real damage. But your story doesn't end with failure. It begins with rising. You get to redefine what success looks like on your terms. You get to design a life that honors your needs and celebrates your differences. You get to be whole.

- You are not too late. You are not too much.
- You are right on time. And you are not alone.

Chapter 3

Adhd & Autism Are Not Just For White Boys

For far too long, the public image of ADHD and autism has been dominated by one narrative: the hyperactive white boy bouncing off classroom walls or the socially awkward white boy obsessed with trains or computers. This narrow stereotype has shaped everything from diagnostic criteria to school interventions and left countless others invisible.

But neurodivergence doesn't have a race, gender, or socioeconomic status. ADHD and autism show up in Black and brown kids, in immigrant families, in girls who were "too quiet" instead of "too loud," in queer teens, in single moms, in people working two jobs to survive. It's always been here just misinterpreted, mislabeled, or missed entirely.

This section challenges the outdated frameworks that have excluded so many of us from getting the recognition and support we deserve. It explores how racism, sexism, classism, and ableism intersect to shape who gets diagnosed and who gets left behind. It invites us to widen the lens, see neurodivergence in all its forms, and center the voices silenced for too long.

ADHD and autism are not just for white boys. They never were. We were here the whole time. It's time the world saw us.

Cultural Masking And Survival Tactics

Before many of us had the words "ADHD" or "autism," we felt that quiet, persistent sense of being different too much or not enough, always a beat behind or ten steps ahead, misunderstood, overcorrected, or invisible. But rather than being seen and supported, we were often expected to blend in, behave, and make it work. So we did what we had to do we *masked*.

Masking is hiding your neurodivergent traits to appear more "normal." It's not always conscious. It starts early, especially if you're a woman, BIPOC, or both. You watch, study, and mimic what others do. You learn to smile when overwhelmed, make eye contact when it feels unnatural, and nod in agreement even when confused or overstimulated. You edit your tone, words, body language, and volume. You try to be "just enough" not loud, quiet, weird, or intense.

But cultural masking goes even deeper. It's not just about fitting into neurotypical norms it's about surviving in a world that sees your identity as a threat, a burden, or a problem to fix.

1. The Pressure To Represent

If you're the only one or one of the few BIPOC folks in a space, you may feel pressure to be *the good one.* The smart one. The one who doesn't cause trouble. That pressure makes masking feel less like a choice and more like a necessity. You don't want to confirm stereotypes. You don't want to make your community "look bad." You learn to shrink yourself, filter your words, and out-perform just to be seen as "equal."

If you're neurodivergent *and* from a marginalized background, you're constantly navigating two realities: managing your brain's unique wiring and managing how the world perceives your identity. That's a heavy cognitive and emotional load, especially without language or validation.

2. The Survival Skills We Mistook For Personality

Many of us developed entire identities around coping mechanisms. Being "the overachiever," "the perfectionist," "the quiet one," or "the helper" wasn't just personality it was protection. We found ways to fly under the radar or prove our value so we wouldn't be targeted, punished, or left out.

You became the kid who always followed the rules, even when they didn't make sense. The teen who laughed along even when you didn't get the joke. The adult who managed everyone's schedules while secretly forgetting your appointments. The person who apologized for everything and asked for nothing.

Nicci Brochard & Dr. Ben Chuba

These survival tactics helped us stay safe in a world not designed for our brains. But over time, they can disconnect us from who we are. We forget what we enjoy, what we need, what our natural rhythms feel like. We've been performing for so long that we don't know where the mask ends and the self begins.

3. The Cost Of Masking

Masking works until it doesn't. Eventually, the cost catches up to you. Burnout. Anxiety. Depression. Identity loss. Emotional numbness. Many late-diagnosed folks look back and realize they weren't actually "fine" they were exhausted, confused, and barely holding it together.

Masking isn't harmless. It takes immense mental energy to constantly monitor yourself, translate your thoughts into socially acceptable language, override your natural instincts, suppress stimming, redirect your attention, or force yourself into environments that overwhelm you. This kind of performance isn't sustainable. It can lead to emotional shutdowns, chronic stress, and even physical illness.

4. Unmasking Isn't Instant Or Easy

After diagnosis, many people talk about wanting to "unmask" to live more authentically. But unmasking is a process, not a switch. For many of us, the mask was welded on in childhood. It protected us from ridicule, rejection, and punishment. It kept us alive in households or communities where being different wasn't safe.

Unmasking means slowly, gently peeling back the layers. It means asking questions like: *What do I like? How do I express myself when no one's watching? What's my natural rhythm for rest, movement, focus, or play?* It's relearning yourself in real-time.

It also means setting boundaries sometimes for the first time. It means disappointing people who benefited from your performance. It might mean facing hard truths about your upbringing, relationships, or work life. On the other hand, however, discomfort is something powerful: *freedom.*

5. We Deserve To Be Our Full Selves

We didn't mask because we were fake we masked because the world told us we had to. But we deserve more than survival. We deserve joy, Ease, Connection, Community, Rest.

You don't have to earn your right to be different. You don't need to justify why the "standard way" doesn't work for you. You get to take off the mask, little by little, and discover who you've been underneath it all along.

Your neurodivergence is not a flaw, and your culture is not a barrier. Together, they make you powerful. And it's time the world made space for *all* of you.

Misdiagnosis, Under diagnosis, And Racial/Sexist Bias In Healthcare

The healthcare system is supposed to help and give us answers and support when something feels off. But for many neurodivergent women and BIPOC individuals, it's where we first learned that being unseen, unheard, or misunderstood was just part of the deal. When you finally worked up the courage to say something's wrong maybe you were overwhelmed, anxious, forgetful, constantly exhausted the response was often dismissive, patronizing, or flat-out wrong.

Too many people were misdiagnosed or never diagnosed. The reason isn't individual error it's baked into the system itself.

1. How Bias Shapes The Diagnostic Process

The truth is the medical and psychological systems we depend on are not objective. Cultural assumptions about race, gender, and behavior deeply influence them. Historically, ADHD and autism have been diagnosed using criteria based on studies of white, cisgender boys. Their external, disruptive, and easily observable symptoms became the "gold standard." But that's not how neurodivergence looks for everyone.

Women and girls often present with internalized symptoms. Instead of acting out, we zone out. We don't lash out; we hold it in. Instead of hyperactivity, we get anxiety. And that leads to doctors and therapists mislabeling us with depression, borderline personality disorder, generalized anxiety, or even bipolar disorder anything but ADHD or autism. Now add race to the equation.

BIPOC individuals are often judged through a different lens altogether. Black children with ADHD may be labeled as oppositional or aggressive. Latina girls may be told they're emotional or dramatic. Asian folks are expected to be quiet, obedient, and high-achieving so their struggles go unnoticed. Indigenous and immigrant populations are rarely studied at all. These stereotypes are so ingrained that even well-meaning providers can't always see past them.

So, while white boys were getting support plans and diagnoses in elementary school, the rest of us were being told to "just try harder," "be more respectful," or "stop overreacting."

2. Why So Many Of Us Were Misdiagnosed

Misdiagnosis happens when doctors recognize the symptoms but don't connect them to the correct cause. If you came into a clinic as a woman saying you're tired, scattered, anxious, and emotional, the doctor likely chalked it up to hormones, motherhood, burnout, or trauma. You were probably prescribed an antidepressant and sent on your way.

The same goes for autism. Many of us were diagnosed with social anxiety or told we were "too sensitive," "rigid," or "emotionally unstable" when we were autistic people navigating an overstimulating, confusing, and invalidating world.

You might've even believed the diagnosis initially, after all, something *was* wrong. But the treatments didn't work. You didn't feel seen. Something still didn't click. You weren't the problem. The diagnosis was.

3. Underdiagnosis Isn't A Coincidence, It's A Pattern

Underdiagnosis means people who should receive a diagnosis never do. Again, it's not random it's systemic.

BIPOC communities face multiple barriers to diagnosis: lack of access to culturally competent providers, language and insurance limitations, and mistrust in the medical system (often for good reason, given its history of exploitation and neglect). Even when we speak up, we're usually brushed off, labeled as "non-compliant," "too complex," or told we're just looking for a label or medication.

Gender bias also plays a significant role. Girls are expected to be quiet, agreeable, and nurturing so when we struggle, it's often internalized and hidden. Many of us become high-functioning on the outside and wholly overwhelmed inside. But no one thinks of digging deeper because we're "doing fine" by external standards.

This leads to delayed diagnoses sometimes by decades. It's not unusual for neurodivergent women and BIPOC individuals to get diagnosed in their late 20s, 30s, 40s, or beyond. And by then, we've already experienced years sometimes a lifetime of feeling broken, confused, or ashamed.

4. The Psychological Toll Of Not Being Seen

The consequences of misdiagnosis and underdiagnosis are not just clinical they're emotional, relational, and spiritual. When you go years without an accurate explanation for your struggles, you start to internalize the blame. You think you're just lazy, Difficult, Flaky, Too sensitive, Not trying hard enough.

You compare yourself to others and wonder why everyday life feels like a marathon while they're just strolling. You question your memory, your judgment, your worth. And each time a provider brushes you off, that wound gets deeper.

For BIPOC individuals, this is compounded by cultural pressures to be strong, not to show weakness, and to handle it all without complaint. Admitting you need help is hard enough being told you don't qualify for it can feel devastating.

5. The Way Forward: Advocacy, Awareness, And Justice

The good news? More people are starting to speak up. Late-diagnosed folks share their stories, break the silence, and change the narrative. Grassroots organizations are pushing for more inclusive research and culturally competent care. Therapists and doctors are beginning to unlearn outdated assumptions and listen more closely. But we still have a long way to go.

We need diagnostic tools for race, gender, and cultural differences. We need more BIPOC and neurodivergent providers. We need training programs that challenge bias instead of reinforcing it. We need to normalize late diagnosis not as a failure, but as a valid and often necessary part of adult life. If you were misdiagnosed, you're not alone. If you were overlooked for years, it wasn't your fault. And if you only understand yourself, there is still time to heal, grow, and thrive.

This isn't just about healthcare it's about justice. It's about believing that our stories deserve to be told, and our needs deserve to be met. Because ADHD and autism don't look one way. And neither does healing.

How Your Identity Impacts Your Neurodivergence Experience

Neurodivergence doesn't happen in a vacuum. It doesn't exist apart from race, gender, culture, class, or sexuality. Who you are, how you move through the world, how others see you, and how you've been taught to see yourself shapes every part of your experience. Your neurodivergence isn't separate from your identity. It *intersects* with it.

Being ADHD or autistic already makes you different in a world designed for neurotypical norms. But when you add other marginalized identities being Black, brown, Indigenous, an immigrant, a woman, trans, queer, poor those differences are filtered through layers of cultural expectations, biases, and survival strategies. Suddenly, it's not just about your brain wiring. It's about navigating a world never built with *you* in mind.

For many of us, this meant learning early on that we had to work twice as hard to be taken half as seriously. Struggling with attention, memory, social cues, or executive function wasn't just "difficult" it was dangerous.

It could mean being seen as rude, disrespectful, incompetent, untrustworthy, or even threatening. And so we became masters at adapting, overcompensating, and masking, not just to fit in but to stay safe.

Cultural identity plays a massive role in how neurodivergence is expressed, perceived, and treated. In many communities of color, mental health is still heavily stigmatized. Neurodivergence may not be a recognized, neutral, or empowering concept. You may have grown up hearing things like "You're just lazy," "You need discipline," or "Stop acting weird." Struggles were often moralized or dismissed "pray about it," "toughen up," "act right." Seeking support could be seen as weak, privileged, or shameful.

There's often an unspoken rule in immigrant households: we don't have the luxury to be different. There's pressure to succeed, assimilate, and carry the dreams of the generations before you. So when your brain doesn't cooperate, when you can't stay organized, struggle in school, or shut down under pressure, it can feel like betrayal like you're failing not just yourself but your family and culture, too.

Gender plays a role in all of this. Women and girls are often socialized to be caregivers, please others, suppress their needs and blend into the background. So, when a girl is struggling with attention, sensory overload, or social confusion, she may go unnoticed. She may seem shy, daydreamy, sensitive, or anxious. The signs of neurodivergence are there but they're hidden under layers of performance. And because so many diagnostic tools were built around male expressions of ADHD and autism, girls and women often fall through the cracks entirely.

Then there's the experience of being queer or trans and neurodivergent. For some, queerness and neurodivergence are deeply intertwined both involve pushing against rigid norms and expectations. However, being part of multiple marginalized groups also means carrying various forms of social and internalized pressure. You may have spent your whole life trying to decode rules that were never made for you. And that decoding of gender, of neurotypical behavior, of cultural norms can be exhausting.

This intersectional reality means that no two neurodivergent journeys are the same. Your background, community, and identity influence how your traits are interpreted. A Black girl who's overwhelmed and shutting down in class might be called defiant. A white boy doing the same might be flagged for evaluation. A Latina woman struggling to stay organized might be told she's just stressed. An Asian child who's masking their autistic traits might be labeled as "obedient" and never get the support they need. The same characteristics can be read differently depending on *who* is displaying them.

It also impacts how you see yourself. If you've never seen anyone like you talk openly about ADHD or autism, it's easy to think it can't apply. If the only stories you've heard are of white men with Silicon Valley success or quirky teenage boys in movies, you may not recognize yourself in those narratives. You may assume your struggles are just personal failings and that you're just weird. Or broken, Or bad, But the truth is, you were never broken. You were just unseen.

Understanding your neurodivergence through the lens of identity is powerful. It gives context to your experience. It helps explain why it took so long to get answers or why you're still searching. It enables you to rewrite the narrative from shame and confusion to clarity, compassion, and cultural awareness. You don't just have ADHD or autism. You have *your* version of it shaped by the complexity of your life. And that version deserves recognition. It deserves care. It deserves space to exist and evolve.

Owning your whole identity your culture, your gender, your queerness, your brain is an act of radical self-trust. It's a way of reclaiming power in a world that told you to hide. When you see yourself clearly, you can finally show up as your whole self not a masked, minimized version for someone else's comfort. Your identity isn't an obstacle to understanding your neurodivergence. It's the key.

Chapter 4

"Ok, Now What?" Life Right After Diagnosis

Getting a diagnosis of ADHD or autism in adulthood is like finally being handed the missing piece of a lifelong puzzle. Things start to click. Memories get reinterpreted. The emotional chaos, the social misfires, the overwhelm it all starts to *make sense.* For a moment, there's relief. Validation, Even joy. But then, almost as quickly, another feeling creeps in: *now what?* Because the diagnosis is only the beginning.

No one tells you what happens after the paperwork is filed and the label is official. You walk out of the psychologist's office or close your laptop if it was a telehealth call and suddenly, you're left with your entire life to re-examine. You might feel like your world shifted on its axis, even if everything around you looks the same. There's no step-by-step handbook, no magical transformation. Just...you. Still you. But with a new lens.

This chapter is for that moment. The one right after the "aha." When you've got more questions than answers. When emotions swing from validation to grief to anger to a kind of cautious hope. When you're trying to figure out how to talk about it, who to tell, what to change, and how to live differently now that you finally have the language.

You're not alone in this messy middle. That feeling of "what now?" is part of the process. It's not a detour it's the path. And while there's no perfect roadmap, there *are* ways forward. This chapter will help you begin to chart yours with honesty, self-compassion, and the knowledge that it's OK to take your time.

Where Do I Even Start?

So you've been diagnosed with ADHD or autism or both and now you're sitting with this huge, life-changing truth. It's exciting, it's validating... and also wholly overwhelming. You might be thinking, "Where do I even begin?" That's normal. When everything you thought you knew about yourself is being reframed, the idea of "starting" can feel almost too big.

This chapter is here to help you slow it down, take a breath, and begin step by step. There's no one "right" way to do this, but here are some places you might want to start:

1. Let Yourself Feel Everything

Before jumping into research or overhauling your routines, permit yourself to *feel*. Diagnosis often comes with emotional whiplash: relief, grief, anger, confusion, clarity, and everything in between. You might mourn the version of yourself you were trying so hard to fix. You might feel rage at the years you were misunderstood. Or you might feel deep gratitude for finally having a name for what you've always sensed.

There's no deadline for processing. This is a massive shift, and whatever you're feeling is valid. Write it out. Talk to someone you trust. Cry if you need to. Celebrate if you want to. Emotional processing *is* part of starting.

2. Learn At Your Own Pace

After diagnosis, a lot of people go into research mode. You may stay up late reading articles, watching neurodivergent TikToks, or trying to understand every symptom and nuance. That can be empowering but it can also be overwhelming. Information overload is real, especially when it's about *you*.

Start small. Pick one or two sources that feel aligned with your identity and values. Books by neurodivergent authors, podcasts, or support groups can be a good entry point. And remember you don't need to know everything at once. This is a lifelong journey, not a crash course.

3. Revisit Your Past With Compassion

One of the most transformative and painful parts of a late diagnosis is looking back at your life with a new understanding. Suddenly, things that never made sense start to align: the meltdowns you were shamed for, the "laziness" that was executive dysfunction, the friendships that never quite clicked. It's easy to fall into regret or "what ifs." What if someone had caught this sooner? What if you'd gotten the support you needed? What if things had been different?

Be gentle with yourself here. You did the best you could with what you knew. That younger version of you survived without the language, without the tools. That's resilience. Now, you get to start making peace with the past by offering yourself the compassion you may never have received.

4. Get Curious About Your Real Needs

Most of us, especially women and BIPOC, have spent years shaping ourselves to fit into neurotypical spaces work, school, and relationships without ever stopping to ask what *we* need. Now is the time to get curious.

Are you more sensitive to noise or lights than you realized? Do you need more time alone than you were taught was acceptable? Are rigid routines comforting or constricting for you? What helps you focus music, silence, movement? You don't need to force yourself to live the way others do. This is your opportunity to start designing a life that supports your brain instead of constantly fighting it.

5. Consider Who You Want To Tell And When

Disclosing your diagnosis is personal, and there's no pressure to share it before you're ready. Some people feel empowered by being open; others need time to sit with the diagnosis privately. You might tell close friends, your partner, your boss, or you might not tell anyone for a while. All of that is OK.

When you do decide to talk about it, having language prepared can help: "I've been diagnosed with ADHD, which helps explain a lot about how I process things. I'm still learning what that means for me." You don't owe anyone the whole story, only what *you* feel safe sharing.

6. Find Or Build Community

This journey doesn't have to be solitary. Others are navigating similar paths, and connecting with them can be incredibly healing. Whether through online forums, group chats, support circles, or social media, the community reminds you *that you're not alone.*

When you see people who look like you, who come from your background, and who are thriving while neurodivergent, something shifts. It gives you permission to thrive, too.

7. Focus On Sustainable Support, Not Quick Fixes

You might feel pressure to "fix" everything now that you have a diagnosis. But this isn't about becoming "better" in the eyes of the world it's about finding tools that support you. That could mean therapy with a neurodivergent-affirming provider, executive function coaching, medication, sensory aids, or changes in your routine. Start small one new tool at a time. The goal isn't perfection it's support.

Diagnosis is the door, not the destination. Starting can be messy, slow, and nonlinear and that's OK. You don't have to figure it all out right away. What matters is that you've arrived at a truth about yourself. And from here, everything is possible. You're not starting over you're starting *for real.*

Sorting Through Labels, Symptoms, And Self-Perception

Getting a diagnosis of ADHD or autism in adulthood can feel like finally being handed the key to your brain but the door it opens leads to a hallway of even more questions. You start to unravel years of internalized beliefs, personality traits, and coping mechanisms, and suddenly, you're faced with the challenge of sorting through what's "you," what's a symptom, what's a survival skill, and what's the result of years of masking or misunderstanding. It's a lot. But it's also where some of the most profound healing begins.

Let's be real labels are complicated. On the one hand, finally having a name for your struggles can feel like freedom. It validates what you've always known: that you weren't lazy, weird, or too sensitive. There was something real going on. On the other hand, labels can feel limiting, especially when they come with years of stigma and misinformation attached.

Many of us grew up seeing ADHD and autism portrayed in very narrow ways usually white, male, and either hyperactive or socially disconnected. So, when we finally get a diagnosis, it can be hard to reconcile our lived experiences with what we thought these conditions looked like. You may start wondering: *Am I "really" autistic if I've always had friends? Can I have ADHD if I get good grades?* These questions stem from outdated stereotypes, not the truth.

Sorting through your neurodivergence means learning to separate the noise of cultural narratives from the actual science and, more importantly, from your *lived experience*. It means recognizing that ADHD and autism show up differently in women, BIPOC folks, and LGBTQ+ individuals. It means seeing that symptoms often manifest in subtler, more internal ways perfectionism, overthinking, chronic fatigue from masking, social burnout, difficulty with transitions, and a deep sense of "otherness" that's been with you as long as you can remember. It's not just about identifying traits. It's about rethinking the story you've been told about who you are.

Maybe you were labeled "the quiet one" when you were overwhelmed by social dynamics you didn't know how to navigate. Perhaps you were the "overachiever" because masking as competent was the only way to feel safe. Maybe you were called "too emotional " when you were deeply attuned to sensory input or other people's moods.

These aren't just personality quirks they're often adaptations rooted in neurodivergence. But because you weren't diagnosed earlier, you likely interpreted them as personal flaws. Untangling that of re-seeing yourself through a more compassionate lens can feel both disorienting and liberating.

This is also the time when a lot of people start asking, *What's me and what's ADHD/autism?* It's a fair question and an impossible one to answer neatly. Neurodivergence isn't a separate layer you can peel off and examine in isolation. It's woven into how you think, feel, relate, and experience the world. It's part of you but it's not all of you.

Instead of drawing a hard line between identity and diagnosis, try asking: *What's working for me? What feels aligned with my values, my energy, my joy?* You don't need to reject parts of yourself just because they "fit the criteria." And you don't need to keep behaviors that cause harm or burn out just because they've helped you survive.

This is your chance to build a more intentional self-image. To sort through internalized shame and cultural expectations, start choosing what you want to carry forward. Maybe being hyper-verbal and info-dumping is something you've been shamed for but what if it's also a strength? Perhaps you've always struggled with starting tasks, and instead of blaming yourself, you can now approach it as an executive function challenge and look for strategies, not shame.

Diagnosis doesn't give you a fixed identity it gives you language. Language to understand yourself better. Language to advocate for what you need. Language to connect with others who share your experience. And with that language, you get to reintroduce yourself to yourself.

Not as broken. Not as behind. However, as someone who was always doing the best they could in a world that didn't give them the right tools or words,

Sorting through your traits and self-perception after diagnosis is not a one-time process. It's a gradual peeling back of layers. Some days, you'll feel empowered, and other days, you'll feel like you're unraveling. Both are part of the work.

Just remember you are not your symptoms, struggles, or the negative labels others put on you. You are a complex person navigating your path with a clearer understanding of yourself than ever before. And that's a powerful place to start.

Dealing With Your Inner Critic (And Others' Opinions)

Getting a late diagnosis of ADHD or autism often triggers a flood of emotions but one of the most persistent and sneaky ones is shame. Whether it shows up as an internal voice telling you you're "too much," "not enough," or "making it up," or from the judgments of others, dealing with criticism especially from within is one of the most complex parts of post-diagnosis life. Here's how to begin recognizing, challenging, and quieting those voices.

1. Recognize The Inner Critic For What It Is

Your inner critic is not the truth. It's the voice of past conditioning. It's the teacher who said you weren't trying hard enough, the parent who told you to stop being dramatic, the boss who called you lazy, the friend who didn't understand why you canceled again.

This voice has been with you for so long that it may feel like your own. But it's not. It's a collection of other people's discomfort, misunderstandings, and expectations. It's rooted in ableism, sexism, racism, and classism and a society that values productivity and perfection over well-being and authenticity.

The first step is to notice it. Catch it in the act. "You're so disorganized." "You never get anything done." "No wonder people get frustrated with you." When those thoughts show up, pause. Ask: *Whose voice is that?*

2. Replace Shame With Curiosity

Shame says, "You're bad." Curiosity asks, "What's going on?" When your inner critic kicks in after you forget an appointment, get overstimulated at a social event, or freeze on a work task, try approaching it like a scientist instead of spiraling into blame: *Why did this happen? What does my brain need right now? What support was missing?*

For example, you may have missed the appointment because your brain doesn't register time like others. That meltdown may be from sensory overload, not weakness. Maybe procrastination was anxiety or executive dysfunction, not laziness. Curiosity leads to understanding. Understanding leads to compassion. And compassion is the antidote to shame.

3. Talk Back (Yes, Literally)

Once you've identified your inner critic, start talking back to it out loud, if necessary. When it says, "You should be better at this by now," you can say, "Actually, I just got the right tools. I'm learning."

When it whispers, "People won't take you seriously," respond with, "People's opinions don't define my reality." It might feel silly initially, but this kind of self-talk is powerful. You've spent years absorbing negative messages you can rewrite them in your voice.

4. Reframe "Failure" Through A Neurodivergent Lens

The world teaches us that success looks like consistency, efficiency, and ease. But if you're neurodivergent, success might look like flexibility, creativity, or simply *getting through the day* without shutting down. That's not failure it's resilience.

If you forgot to eat until 3 PM but eventually remembered, that's progress. If you set a boundary with a friend who drains your energy, that's growth. If you asked for help instead of masking, that's strength. Reframe your wins. Celebrate what neurotypicals might overlook. You're not failing you're adapting to a world that wasn't built for you.

5. Create An Internal Ally

Alongside the inner critic, begin building another voice: your inner advocate. This is the part of you that knows you've worked hard, sees your growth, and celebrates your efforts even when results don't look "perfect."

You might name this voice, journal from their perspective, or imagine what they'd say in moments of struggle. It sounds like a friend, a therapist, a future version of you, or a beloved community elder who *gets it*. Let that voice speak louder over time.

6. Set Boundaries With External Critics

Sometimes, the loudest critics aren't in your head they're people in your life. Friends who say, "Everyone's a little ADHD." Family members who think you're being dramatic coworkers who question your accommodations.

You do *not* owe anyone a breakdown of your diagnosis. You do not have to educate people who are unwilling to learn. You can say:

- "That comment isn't helpful."

- "I'm still processing my diagnosis, and I need support not skepticism."

- "This is real for me, even if it's new for you."

You have the right to protect your peace.

7. Build A Circle That Reflects Your Reality

External validation is the best cure for internalized shame from people who truly see you.

Whether it's online neurodivergent communities, local support groups, or one or two close friends, find people who understand your reality. Whoever celebrate your wins, validate your pain, and remind you that your brain is not a problem to be fixed. Surround yourself with voices that uplift you and let their words become your own.

You've lived so much of your life under the weight of expectations that didn't fit you. Your inner critic is loud because it grew in a world that rewarded silence, sameness, and self-denial. But now you have new tools, new language, and new truths.

You're allowed to speak kindly to yourself. You're allowed to grow without shame. You're allowed to be exactly who you are. And that critic? It's not in charge anymore.

Chapter 5

Unmasking And Reclaiming Your Truth

For many late-diagnosed neurodivergent folks especially women, BIPOC, and those at the intersections of multiple marginalized identities masking becomes second nature long before we even know we're doing it. It's the smiling when we're overwhelmed. The eye contact we force. Mimicking "normal" behavior to blend in, stay safe, and survive. We become experts at it so good, in fact, that sometimes we lose sight of where the mask ends and where we begin.

But once the diagnosis comes, something shifts. The question is no longer, "How do I keep performing this version of myself?" It becomes, "Who am I *really*, beneath it all?"

This chapter is about the powerful and often uncomfortable unmasking process. It's not just about dropping social scripts or stimming freely (though those things matter, too). It's about examining the parts of yourself you've hidden, denied, or reshaped to meet others' expectations. It's about allowing yourself to take up space, move differently, speak honestly, and reconnect with your authentic rhythms and needs.

Unmasking isn't instant. It's a layered, emotional process that brings fear, grief, freedom, and relief. But as you slowly shed the armor you didn't know you were wearing, you make room for something more profound: *authenticity*. This is where reclamation begins not just of your neurodivergence, but of your full, complex self.

What Masking Looked Like In Your Life

For many of us who received our ADHD or autism diagnosis later in life, the concept of "masking" hits hard. It's like suddenly realizing you've been playing a role for decades one that kept you safe, accepted, or even praised but left you exhausted and disconnected from your true self. The mask becomes so normalized that it feels like part of your personality.

But now that you're learning more about your neurodivergence, you're starting to recognize just how deeply that mask has shaped your life. Let's break down what masking might have looked like in your life, whether you realized it or not.

1. You Became A Master Chameleon In Social Settings

You studied how others talked, laughed, or reacted and mirrored them to fit in. You learned to nod at the right time, laugh when everyone else laughed (even if you didn't get the joke), and force eye contact, even though it felt unnatural. You might have pre-rehearsed conversations in your head or copied mannerisms from TV shows or people you admire.

Socializing wasn't intuitive it was performance. And after every interaction, you likely felt drained, anxious, or like you needed hours (or days) to recover.

2. **You Overachieved To Distract From Your Struggles**

Whether in school, at work, or even in friendships, you worked *twice* as hard to avoid being seen as "difficult," "slow," or "lazy." You pushed through burnout. You obsessed over details. You volunteered to lead projects or kept your space extra tidy not necessarily because it came easy, but because it helped you feel "good enough" or "in control."

The overachieving wasn't about confidence it was about survival. You hoped that if you kept performing at a high level, no one would notice the areas where you were silently struggling.

3. **You Suppressed Your Stims Or Unusual Behaviors**

You may have had natural tendencies like fidgeting, humming, rocking, tapping, repeating words, or other sensory movements that helped you self-regulate. But at some point, you learned those behaviors were "weird" or "disruptive," so you trained yourself to hide them.

You clenched your hands instead of flapping them, picked your skin in private instead of rocking in public, and repressed physical expressions of excitement, anxiety, or sensory overload. By doing so, you disconnected from your body's natural regulation system.

4. You Played The "Chill" Or "Cool" Version Of Yourself In Relationships

You didn't always speak about your needs or express discomfort. You let people talk over you. You agreed to things you didn't want to do. You tried to be "low-maintenance," even when that meant denying your boundaries or needs.

Whether in friendships, family dynamics, or romantic relationships, you may have played a version of yourself that felt more acceptable or easier to love at the cost of your emotional well-being.

5. You Minimized Or Questioned Your Own Needs

Masking isn't always visible it also happens internally. You gaslight yourself. You told yourself your sensory issues weren't "a big deal." You blamed your executive dysfunction on laziness. You made excuses for your burnout, saying, "Everyone's tired," even when you were clearly on the verge of collapse.

You convinced yourself you'd be "normal if you tried harder." But deep down, you always knew something wasn't adding up.

6. **You Learned To Laugh Off The Hurt**

When people made jokes about your quirks or labeled you as "too much," "too sensitive," or "too intense," you laughed along. You turned your confusion or social anxiety into self-deprecating humor. You became the "funny one," the "spacey one," and the "hot mess" to deflect from how deeply misunderstood you felt.

Humor became a shield. It masked the pain of not being seen and gave people a version of you they could accept.

7. **You Lost Sight Of What Was "You" And What Was Performance**

After years or even decades of masking, you might've reached a point where you didn't know what you *liked* or *needed*. Did you genuinely enjoy that loud concert, or were you pretending because everyone else was? Did you pick that career path because it made you feel alive or because it was the "responsible" choice?

Unmasking means starting to ask those questions again. It means returning to yourself, layer by layer, after years of shaping your identity around survival and acceptance.

Masking was never your fault. It was a strategy, a shield, a way to navigate a world that made you feel like your authentic self was "too much" or "not enough." But now that you have a name for it, you have a choice. You can start releasing the mask, bit by bit, and reconnecting with who you were always meant to be. Not all at once. Not perfectly. But intentionally, Honestly, Freely.

Nicci Brochard & Dr. Ben Chuba

You're allowed to be real. You're allowed to take up space. And the more you unmask, the more you'll find your truth underneath waiting for you.

The Cost Of Fitting In

For many late-diagnosed neurodivergent people especially women and BIPOC the drive to "fit in" wasn't about being popular or polished. It was about survival. From a young age, many of us learned that to be accepted, we had to tone ourselves down, hide our differences, and stay in line. We thought we were just being mature, adaptable, and hardworking. We didn't know we were slowly chipping away at our sense of self.

Fitting in might have protected you from ridicule, rejection, or misunderstanding but it came at a cost. And now that you're looking back with clearer eyes, you might be starting to see how much you paid to seem "normal."

1. Emotional Exhaustion Became Your Baseline

Masking and people-pleasing take energy so much energy. You spent years analyzing every social situation, rehearsing your responses, over-correcting your behaviors, and anticipating others' reactions. Even things that came easily to other people small talk, group projects, office meetings took a toll on your nervous system.

By the time you got home, you were often drained, irritable, or numb. But because this was your "normal," you likely blamed yourself for not having enough stamina or assumed everyone felt this way. It never occurred to you that you were doing *extra emotional labor* just to be tolerated.

2. You Sacrificed Authentic Connections

When you constantly edit yourself to be more palatable, you're not truly connecting with people you're connecting *through* a mask. And when your relationships are built on that version of you, it's hard to feel truly seen or loved.

You might have found yourself surrounded by people who "liked" you but didn't *know* you. Or you might have kept your distance from others because the fear of being "found out" was too great. Real intimacy requires vulnerability, but fitting in often requires hiding your most vulnerable parts.

3. Your Mental Health Suffered

Living in a constant state of performance, self-censorship, and overcompensation isn't sustainable. Over time, this can lead to anxiety, depression, burnout, and even dissociation. The effort to push through environments that overwhelm you without tools, support, or understanding leaves a profound impact.

Many of us internalized the message that we were failing at life because we couldn't keep up. In reality, we were unsupported neurodivergent people trying to meet standards that were never designed with us in mind. That's not failure that's trauma

.

4. **You Developed Shame Around Your Needs**

When fitting in becomes the goal, anything that sets you apart can feel like a flaw. Instead of honoring your sensory sensitivities, executive function challenges, or social overwhelm, you learned to hide them. You taught yourself not to need breaks, not to ask questions, not to make a scene.

Eventually, you started believing the problem wasn't the environment but *you*. You blamed yourself for needing accommodations, feeling "too much," or struggling with tasks others found easy. And that shame is heavy. It lingers long after the moment has passed.

5. **You Missed Out On Joy**

Maybe you avoided things that would've brought you joy dancing without self-consciousness, diving into a deep special interest, asking that weird but brilliant question because you were afraid of judgment. Maybe you said no to opportunities or friendships that felt "risky" because they required you to show your authentic self.

Fitting in often means silencing your enthusiasm, flattening your curiosity, and ignoring your instincts. But those parts of you bring color and aliveness to life. The longer you hide them, the dimmer life becomes.

6. **You Built A Life That Didn't Quite Fit**

When you make choices based on what's expected rather than what's authentic, you can end up with a life that looks "successful" on the outside but feels hollow. The career you chose to prove you were capable. The relationship felt "safe" but stifling. The routines that look good on paper but don't nourish you.

Now, with your diagnosis in hand, you're beginning to untangle all the shoulds from the wants. And that's a scary but beautiful process: recognizing that fitting in might've helped you survive, but it never helped you *thrive*.

7. You Lost Time But You're Not Too Late

One of the most brutal truths to confront post-diagnosis is the time you feel like you've lost. Time spent being someone else time spent in self-doubt. Time spent chasing a version of "normal" that was never meant for you.

And yet here you are. You've made it to the part where you can *choose* what fitting in is worth and what belonging means. You get to take back your time, your joy, your voice. You get to build a life that fits *you*, not vice versa.

The cost of fitting in was real. But now that you see it clearly, you don't have to keep paying it. You can take up space in your whole, unfiltered, neurodivergent truth. You were never too weird. You were too *real* for a world that didn't know how to hold you. And now, you're learning to hold yourself.

Relearning Authenticity: Awkward, Liberating, Necessary

There's a strange moment after a late diagnosis when the mask starts to slip, and you realize you don't know who you are without it. You curated your behaviors,

Nicci Brochard & Dr. Ben Chuba

reactions, and personality for so long to match what others expected from you.

You became adaptable, agreeable, high-functioning, resilient all the things the world praised, but none necessarily reflected your most authentic self. Now, with the clarity of an ADHD or autism diagnosis, you're facing an unfamiliar and messy task: relearning authenticity. And yes, it's awkward, uncomfortable, and vulnerable. But it's also deeply, undeniably necessary.

Relearning authenticity starts with unlearning performance. That means noticing how often you still scan the room before speaking your mind or how you instinctively say "I'm fine" when you're not. It means catching yourself, minimizing your needs, pretending not to care, laughing at jokes that sting, and accepting less than you deserve because those behaviors used to keep you safe. The hard truth is, they probably did protect you at some point. But now, they're just keeping you from yourself.

This process is awkward because it often means reintroducing yourself to your emotions. You might realize you've spent so much time filtering your reactions that you're not sure what you feel anymore. Happiness might feel muted. Anger might be unfamiliar. Sadness might catch you off guard. But all of it is real, and all of it is worth exploring. You're not too sensitive you're finally *in touch*.

Being authentic also means showing up in ways that might make others uncomfortable. You may stop pretending to be okay with last-minute plans. You may speak up when someone interrupts or asks for accommodations without apologizing. You should sit openly or wear clothes that make your body feel good instead of conforming to what's trendy or expected. These things might feel radical not because they are, but because you've been conditioned to believe they're "too much."

The liberating part? You start to breathe differently. You laugh more freely. You rest without guilt. You stop second-guessing every text, every word, every reaction. You find people who get you, not the edited version. Do you realize that genuine relationships can withstand honesty and the ones that can't? Maybe they were never safe to begin with.

There's liberation in permitting yourself. Permission to say "no," Permission to take longer to process things, Permission to ask questions, need space, express big emotions, and take up space. You no longer need to apologize for being wired differently. You are. And that is not a flaw it's a fact.

Authenticity doesn't mean you never mask again. There will still be spaces especially for BIPOC, women, and other marginalized folks where safety depends on being strategic. Authenticity doesn't erase the systems we live in. It just helps you move through them with more clarity and intention. You begin to choose when and how you mask rather than do it automatically. That choice is powerful. That choice is freedom.

And yes, it can be lonely at first. People who benefitted from your compliance may not understand the shift. They might say you've "changed." But you haven't changed you're just showing up as your whole self, and not everyone has earned access to that version of you. That's okay. The more you unmask, the more you'll find the ones who love you *because* of your truth, not despite it.

This isn't a linear journey. Some days, authenticity feels easy. On other days, you'll slip back into old habits, doubt yourself, or question whether this new path is even worth it. That's normal. That's human. Relearning yourself takes time. You're not doing it wrong just because it feels hard.

But keep going. Keep asking: "What do *I* need right now?" Keep honoring what feels true, even when it's unexpected. Keep choosing presence over perfection. Bit by bit, you're becoming more you and there's nothing awkward about that.

Liberation isn't always loud. Sometimes, it looks like leaving a party without explaining yourself. Sometimes, it sounds like your own laugh, unfiltered. Sometimes, it feels like coming home to your body for the first time in years. Relearning authenticity might be awkward. It might be liberating. But above all, it's necessary. Because you deserve to know who you are beyond the roles, the rules, and the mask. And that version of you? They are worth meeting.

Chapter 6

Rewriting Your Story

For so long, your narrative may have been defined by other people's expectations what they thought you should be, how they believed you should act, and the standards you were supposed to meet. You might have internalized these ideas, telling yourself you weren't quite enough, that something was "wrong" with you, or that you were "too much." But after a late diagnosis of ADHD or autism, you're waking up to the realization that those old scripts no longer serve you.

Rewriting your story doesn't mean erasing your past. It doesn't mean pretending that the struggles, misunderstandings, or heartbreaks didn't happen. It simply means shifting your perspective. It means reframing the narrative so that you can see yourself as a resilient, adaptive person who's done their best with limited resources. It means acknowledging that your neurodivergence isn't a flaw it's a fundamental part of who you are and brings strengths.

This chapter is about reclaiming agency over your life's narrative. You'll learn how to challenge the negative stories that have held you captive and rewrite them with a sense of empowerment. You'll discover that you are not defined by how others have viewed or treated you. You are the author of your own story, and the most potent part of this process is that you get to decide how you show up moving forward.

Rewriting your story is not about perfection it's about authenticity. It's about exploring without the weight of past limitations or external pressures. This is your chance to step into a new, more compassionate version of yourself. It's time to start writing the next chapter, one that's rooted in truth, acceptance, and growth.

Rethinking Your Past With New Eyes

When you receive a late diagnosis of ADHD or autism, it's like being given a new pair of glasses. Suddenly, the world you've known, including your life experiences, looks different. Things that once seemed confusing, painful, or isolating now make sense in a new light. And with that clarity comes the overwhelming task of rethinking your past.

You begin to see the moments, relationships, and decisions in a new way not as failures or personal shortcomings, but as signs of neurodivergence that were never understood or acknowledged. Here's how you can start rethinking your past with new eyes.

1. Reframing Childhood Struggles

For many of us, the realization that we have ADHD, or autism comes after years of struggling with seemingly minor but significant challenges. Perhaps you were the child who couldn't sit still in class or struggled with loud noises, bright lights, or social interactions that others took for granted. In hindsight, you might now recognize those traits as markers of a neurodivergent brain, but at the time, you were likely labeled as difficult, disobedient, or "not trying hard enough."

Rethinking these early years is an essential step in healing. Instead of viewing these challenges as personal failures or a lack of discipline, you can begin to see them for what they were: signs of a brain weird, trying to make sense of a world that wasn't designed for it. Your struggles were never your fault simply a mismatch between your brain and environment. Reframing your childhood in this way can lift the burden of shame you've carried for so long.

2. Understanding Social Struggles In New Ways

As you think back to your school years or early adulthood, social interactions may stand out as moments of confusion or discomfort. You couldn't keep up with the fast-paced conversations or didn't understand the social cues that others seemed to pick up effortlessly. You might have been the one who was left out or struggled with making friends. You might have tried to fit in by pretending to be something you weren't, or perhaps you withdrew because it all felt overwhelming.

With a new understanding of your neurodivergence, these social struggles have a different meaning. Rather than blaming yourself for not "trying hard enough" or "failing at life," you can begin to see that your social difficulties were a natural outcome of being a neurodivergent person in a world that often favors social conformity. Social situations were never about your worth they were about mismatched expectations and a lack of support for your unique needs.

3. **Reinterpreting Academic And Professional Setbacks**

Perhaps you were an overachiever in school, constantly pushing yourself to meet high expectations but still falling short in certain areas, like time management, staying organized, or keeping up with assignments. Or maybe you struggled with executive function challenges that left you feeling inadequate or overwhelmed. You may have received feedback that you were "too scattered" or "disorganized," adding to the internalized pressure to perform.

Now, with the knowledge of your ADHD or autism, you can reinterpret those academic and professional setbacks. They were not evidence of laziness or a lack of intelligence they were signs of a mismatch between your natural strengths and the traditional systems that didn't accommodate your neurodivergent brain. By seeing those past challenges through the lens of neurodivergence, you can stop internalizing them as personal shortcomings and start recognizing the resilience it took to keep going in a world that didn't understand you.

4. Letting Go Of The "What Could Have Been" Narrative

It's easy to fall into the trap of wondering what your life would have been like if you had known about your neurodivergence earlier. "If only I had known, maybe things would have been easier." You might feel frustration or even grief for the opportunities you missed or the challenges you could have avoided. But holding onto this narrative of "what could have been" will only keep you trapped in the past.

Instead, rethinking your past with new eyes means letting go of the illusion that things could have been different. The reality is that your life, your experiences, and your struggles have shaped you into the person you are today. You survived without the needed support, and resilience is a strength, not a weakness. While you can't change the past, you can change how you view it. By embracing your experiences as part of your unique neurodivergent journey, you free yourself from the weight of regret and open up space for self-compassion.

5. Reclaiming Your Story With Empowerment

Rethinking your past with new eyes means taking control of your narrative. It means no longer allowing others to define your worth based on how well you fit into their systems or expectations. You can reclaim your story rooted in authenticity, resilience, and self-acceptance. Your past is not a series of failures or missteps it's a collection of experiences that shaped who you are today.

By viewing your past through the lens of neurodivergence, you can release the shame, guilt, and self-blame that may have held you back for so long. You can begin to see yourself as someone who has faced challenges but has also navigated a world that was not built for her, all while trying to make the best of what was given. That's powerful. That's worth celebrating.

Rewriting your past with new eyes doesn't erase the pain or difficulty you've experienced it simply gives you the perspective you need to see it for what it truly is: part of your journey. With this new understanding, you can begin to move forward with more compassion for yourself, less judgment, and a stronger sense of self-worth.

Reparenting Yourself: Self-Compassion Over Shame

For many of us, our journey to understanding our neurodivergence is not just about getting a diagnosis it's about learning to care for ourselves in ways that we were never taught. When you realize you've been masking, adapting, and suppressing your true self for years, it can feel like you've been a stranger to yourself for much of your life. The process of "reparenting" yourself, or learning to care for your inner child in ways that nurture and protect you, becomes an essential part of healing.

At the heart of reparenting yourself is the practice of self-compassion. Self-compassion is the antidote to shame, and many of us, especially neurodivergent people, have been deprived of it. For years, we've been taught to push past our struggles, ignore our needs, and minimize our differences. Society especially for women and BIPOC often demands perfection, conformity, and emotional resilience without understanding that these expectations can be damaging and unrealistic.

Reparenting yourself means giving yourself the care, understanding, and nurturing that you may not have received growing up. It's about replacing the harsh, critical voices in your head with kind, supportive, and patient ones. It's a shift from self-criticism to self-acceptance.

1. **Understanding The Impact Of Shame**

For many neurodivergent people, shame has been a constant companion. Shame often arises from believing you are "too much" or "not enough." That whisper tells you something is inherently wrong with you because you don't conform to the world's expectations. It might have started in childhood when you were punished for being "disruptive" in class or reprimanded for not following social cues. As a result, you internalize these messages, leading you to believe your authentic self isn't good enough.

Shame is a powerful force. It convinces you that your neurodivergence is something to hide, something to be fixed, and something that others won't accept. But reparenting yourself is about turning away from this harmful cycle. You start to recognize that your neurodivergence is not something shameful but a part of who you are. By treating yourself with compassion, you can begin to untangle the web of shame woven around your self-worth.

2. Embracing Your Inner Child

Reparenting yourself also means reconnecting with your inner child the part of you that may have been neglected or overlooked during your formative years. The child within you has often been silenced in favor of meeting external expectations. You may have been told to "grow up" quickly or ignore your emotional needs to fit into a world that wasn't designed for you.

You must learn to acknowledge and listen to your inner child to reparent yourself. This child might feel abandoned, misunderstood, or lost. She may have been told that her needs or emotions were too big to handle. You can heal the wounds left from years of neglecting her needs by offering her love, patience, and understanding.

Reparenting involves being kind to yourself, and sometimes that means going back to the basics allowing yourself to play, rest, and feel without judgment. It's letting your inner child know it's okay to be who you are without pretending, performing, or masking. You can express your emotions freely without fear of being dismissed or criticized.

3. Replacing Self-Criticism With Self-Compassion

One of the hardest parts of reparenting is learning to replace self-criticism with self-compassion. You may be so used to berating yourself when things don't go as planned or when you feel overwhelmed that you've been conditioned to see your mistakes or setbacks as failures rather than as learning opportunities or a natural part of being human.

But self-compassion teaches you to respond to yourself with kindness, not judgment. It's about recognizing that you're doing your best with the tools and resources you have. Instead of criticizing yourself for being "too emotional" or "too sensitive," you can begin to acknowledge these traits as part of your neurodivergence. They don't make you weak; they make you unique.

A compassionate approach to yourself doesn't mean letting yourself off the hook for responsibilities or challenging behavior. It does mean treating yourself as you would a loved one offering encouragement, support, and understanding rather than punishment or ridicule.

4. Creating Boundaries With Yourself And Others

Reparenting yourself also involves setting healthy boundaries. It's about recognizing that you can protect your energy and prioritize your needs. Boundaries might initially feel uncomfortable especially if you've spent much of your life trying to please others or conform to external expectations. But learning to say "no" when necessary is an act of self-care.

Part of self-compassion is acknowledging that your energy is finite. You are allowed to say no to things that drain, exhaust, or make you feel unsafe. Setting boundaries with yourself means acknowledging and respecting your limits, permitting yourself to rest, take breaks, or stop pushing through when you're overwhelmed.

It's also about recognizing when others are crossing your boundaries and learning how to assert yourself in a way that protects your well-being. Reparenting yourself means trusting your instincts and speaking up for your needs.

5. **Healing Through Practice**

Reparenting is not something you do once and then move on from. It's an ongoing practice a daily commitment to showing up for yourself with love, patience, and care. It means taking the time to listen to your feelings, recognizing when you're slipping into old patterns of self-criticism, and gently guiding yourself back to self-compassion.

Healing is not linear, and there will be moments when old patterns of shame creep in. But with each step toward self-compassion, you build a foundation of self-love and acceptance that will support you as you navigate the complexities of neurodivergence.

Reparenting yourself is a revolutionary act of self-care and healing. It's about undoing the harm that was done and building a new, nurturing relationship with yourself. As you practice self-compassion over shame, you empower yourself to live authentically and embrace your neurodivergence with confidence.

Letting Go Of The "Lazy, Crazy, Stupid" Narratives

Throughout life, many of us have internalized a series of damaging narratives about ourselves stories that tell us we are "lazy," "crazy," or "stupid" because of how we think, feel, and act. These labels often stem from misunderstanding, from the world's inability to recognize the unique ways our minds work. But when you receive a late diagnosis of ADHD or autism, a decisive shift begins: You start to see these narratives for what they truly are misconceptions, falsehoods, and, most importantly, stories you no longer have to carry.

Letting go of these narratives isn't easy. These labels have been worn for so long that they feel part of your identity. They have shaped your self-worth, your choices, and your relationships. But the moment you recognize that these labels don't define you, liberation begins.

First, the "lazy" narrative. How often have you heard or thought you were lazy because you couldn't keep up with tasks or finish projects on time? This label is usually tied to how society values productivity, efficiency, and completion. For neurodivergent individuals, the struggle to meet these expectations is not about laziness but how the brain processes information, handles tasks, and deals with distractions. With ADHD or autism, completing a task often takes more effort, more energy, and more time. The brain doesn't follow the conventional pathways that make it easy for others to "get it done." But instead of recognizing the effort it takes to stay engaged, many people label us as lazy, whether it's teachers, bosses, or even ourselves.

Letting go of the "lazy" narrative means recognizing that your struggle to stay on track is not a flaw but a sign of how your brain operates. It means understanding that productivity isn't just about doing; it's about doing in a way that aligns with your strengths and accommodates your needs. When you let go of the lazy narrative, you allow yourself to embrace your unique process without self-judgment. You realize that your worth is not tied to how quickly you can check off a to-do list but to how much effort you put into the things that matter to you.

Then there's the "crazy" narrative. How often did you hear or think something was "wrong" with you because you reacted differently to situations or found socializing overwhelming? Frequently, people who have ADHD or autism are misunderstood, especially when it comes to emotional responses or behaviors that deviate from the norm. You might have been told you were too sensitive or emotional or that you "overreacted" to things others didn't bat an eye at. This is where the "crazy" narrative comes from being labeled as mentally unstable simply because your neurodivergence isn't recognized or understood.

Letting go of the "crazy" label means learning to embrace the intensity of your emotions as a reflection of your unique wiring, not as a sign of instability. It means permitting yourself to experience feelings without shame, without trying to suppress or explain them. You are not crazy for feeling deeply. You are not overreacting when the world around you feels too much. These are simply the expressions of a neurodivergent mind trying to process overwhelming stimuli, information, or emotions in a world that wasn't built for it.

And finally, the "stupid" narrative. How many times have you doubted your intelligence because you struggled with organizing your thoughts, staying focused, or retaining information in a way others did? Maybe you've felt ashamed of your difficulty with specific tasks, from remembering details to following through on things that seemed so simple to others. You might have been told that you were "not trying hard enough" or that you weren't as smart as your peers because your brain didn't function in the traditional ways.

These experiences are the foundation of the "stupid" narrative a belief that your mind, somehow, isn't as sharp or capable as others.

Letting go of this narrative is one of the most freeing things you can do. Realizing that ADHD and autism don't correlate to a lack of intelligence is key. People with these neurodivergent traits may struggle with organization or focus, but that doesn't mean they aren't brilliant in other areas. Many neurodivergent individuals possess exceptional talents in creativity, problem-solving, and innovation. Once you let go of the "stupid" label, you can embrace the unique ways your mind works ways that might not align with traditional measures of intelligence but are no less valuable.

Shedding these narratives requires more than intellectual understanding emotional release. It involves forgiving yourself for believing these damaging stories and allowing yourself to see your full potential. These labels have often been reinforced by others teachers, family members, friends, or coworkers but now, it's time to let go of them for good. These are not truths; they are misperceptions born of a lack of understanding.

As you release the "lazy," "crazy," and "stupid" narratives, you replace them with a new story one of resilience, creativity, intelligence, and strength. You begin to see yourself not as someone who has failed but has navigated a challenging world with grace and perseverance. Letting go of these labels doesn't mean you're excusing past difficulties; it means choosing to see those difficulties as part of your growth. It means recognizing that your neurodivergence is not something that limits you it's a part of what makes you unique, complex, and capable.

Letting go of these narratives isn't about becoming perfect or pretending your struggles don't exist. It's about accepting yourself for who you truly are, free from the damaging labels you've carried for far too long. It's about rewriting your story from a place of self-compassion, understanding, and empowerment.

You are not lazy, crazy, or stupid. You are beautifully neurodivergent, and it's time the world saw you that way.

Chapter 7

Relationships, Boundaries & Neurodivergent Love

N avigating relationships as a neurodivergent person whether romantic, familial, or platonic can be both rewarding and challenging. The traditional norms of communication, emotional expression, and social interaction often don't align with how neurodivergent individuals experience the world. ADHD and autism can impact everything from how we connect with others to how we express love and need space.

This chapter explores the complexities of relationships and boundaries in neurodivergent life. For many of us, the challenge isn't about the ability to love but about how we do it, set limits, and communicate our needs. It's about navigating misunderstandings, honoring our emotional experiences, and advocating for ourselves while cultivating meaningful connections. Whether it's learning to communicate your needs more clearly or understanding your emotional responses, this section will offer guidance on building relationships where you can thrive authentically.

Navigating Family, Friendships, And Dating

Navigating family, friendships, and dating as a neurodivergent person can be a complex and deeply personal journey. Whether you have ADHD, autism, or any other neurodivergent trait, these relationships can sometimes feel like a balancing act between wanting connection and managing the challenges that come with being neurodivergent in a world that often doesn't understand how you experience the world. Navigating these spaces requires self-awareness, patience, and frequently reevaluating what it means to connect with others.

Family relationships, in particular, can be one of the most challenging areas for neurodivergent individuals. Family dynamics can carry long-standing expectations and patterns that are hard to break from childhood through adulthood. Perhaps, as a child, you were often misunderstood, or your neurodivergence was not recognized. You may have been labeled as "difficult" or "overemotional" when what you were experiencing was sensory overload or executive function challenges. As an adult, these misunderstandings can persist, especially if your family members have not yet accepted your neurodivergence or continue to push you into old patterns of behavior.

In navigating family dynamics, it's essential to establish healthy boundaries. These may be communicating your needs more explicitly, such as explaining that you need time alone to recharge after family gatherings or setting limits around specific conversations or overwhelming interactions. This can be difficult, mainly if your family is used to particular dynamics or doesn't understand your neurodivergence, but it's essential for your well-being. Part of this process involves advocating for yourself sometimes in ways that might feel uncomfortable but are necessary for your emotional health.

Friendships can offer a different, yet similarly complex, set of challenges. For neurodivergent individuals, friendships may involve navigating unspoken social rules, understanding the give-and-take of reciprocal emotional exchanges, and coping with potential misunderstandings. You're not alone if you've ever felt isolated because you didn't quite "get" a friend's emotional cues or struggled to engage in conversations that seemed to follow unpredictable rhythms. These difficulties can often result in feelings of inadequacy or guilt, leading you to withdraw from social situations altogether.

It's essential to recognize that true friendships those built on mutual respect and understanding don't require you to fit into predefined molds of social behavior. As you become more aware of your neurodivergence, it's important to cultivate friendships that celebrate your unique qualities and accept you for who you are. This may mean seeking out empathetic, patient, and open-minded people about neurodivergence. You might also need to communicate openly with your friends about what works for you in a friendship whether needing more direct communication, extra time to process emotions, or a clear understanding of boundaries. Real friends will listen and adjust, helping you form meaningful, authentic connections.

Dating is where neurodivergence can feel most challenging. The rules of romance, attraction, and emotional intimacy are often unspoken, and for many neurodivergent individuals, they are challenging to navigate without explicit instruction. You might struggle with things like interpreting body language, processing emotions in real-time, or handling the sensory overload of socializing in romantic contexts. The early stages of dating can feel overwhelming as you try to manage the anxiety of newness while also confronting the potential for misunderstanding or rejection based on your neurodivergent traits.

That said, dating as a neurodivergent person also offers opportunities for self-discovery and growth. One of the most important things you can do in navigating romantic relationships is to be upfront about your neurodivergence with potential partners. While it may initially feel intimidating, sharing your neurodivergence can help alleviate misunderstandings and establish a foundation of trust. It allows your partner to understand your needs more clearly and gives you the space to be your true self without fear of being misunderstood or judged.

Setting and respecting boundaries is even more critical when it comes to dating. Your boundaries may look different from those of neurotypical individuals, whether it's around physical touch, communication styles, or the pace of the relationship. Being honest with yourself and potential partners about your needs ensures that you don't compromise your comfort or well-being by fitting in or seeking approval.

Navigating family, friendships, and dating as a neurodivergent individual requires self-awareness, self-advocacy, and the courage to embrace your unique traits. It's about finding and creating relationships where you can be yourself without masking, pretending, and feeling the pressure to conform to societal expectations. These relationships can be profoundly fulfilling when built on mutual respect, empathy, and understanding. It's about discovering your capacity for love, connection, and emotional intimacy on your terms.

Setting Boundaries Without Guilt

Setting boundaries is essential for maintaining emotional and mental well-being, particularly for neurodivergent individuals who may find it more challenging to navigate the demands of the world around them. We set boundaries with ourselves and others to protect our time, energy, and emotional space. However, for many people especially women and BIPOC setting boundaries can come with feelings of guilt, fear, or anxiety. We may worry that setting boundaries will lead to rejection, conflict, or the perception that we are selfish or unreasonable. Yet, boundaries are necessary for healthy relationships and self-care. In this section, we'll explore how to set boundaries with confidence and without guilt while honoring your neurodivergence and emotional needs.

1. Understanding Boundaries And Their Importance

Boundaries are not about shutting people out, rejecting others, or being "cold" or "uncaring." Instead, they are about ensuring that you are not overwhelmed by the needs and expectations of others. For neurodivergent individuals, boundaries may involve specific ways to manage sensory overload, social interactions, or time commitments. For example, you may need quiet time after a social event to recharge or limit the amount of time spent on specific tasks to avoid burnout. Setting boundaries allows you to prioritize your health, energy, and overall well-being without sacrificing yourself.

2. Recognizing The Sources Of Guilt

A big part of setting boundaries without guilt is understanding why guilt arises in the first place. For many, especially in cultures that value selflessness and being "nice," setting boundaries can feel like selfishness. You might worry that saying "no" will disappoint others or make you seem difficult. For neurodivergent people, the pressure to conform to social expectations can feel even more intense. You may have been conditioned to suppress your needs in favor of social harmony or to fit into a world that wasn't designed for you. Recognizing these sources of guilt is the first step in releasing them.

3. Reframing Boundaries As Self-Care

Instead of seeing boundaries as negative or harmful, reframe them as an act of self-care. Establishing boundaries is about prioritizing your mental and emotional health, which, in turn, benefits your relationships and overall quality of life. By setting clear boundaries, you show respect for your needs and ensure that you can be the best version of yourself when engaging with others. Rather than consider boundary-setting a form of rejection, view it as an investment in your well-being. This mindset shift helps alleviate guilt and fosters self-compassion.

4. Start Small And Practice Self-Compassion

Setting boundaries doesn't always have to be a grand, dramatic declaration. It can start with small, everyday decisions. It might be as simple as saying, "I need a break," when you're overwhelmed or telling a friend, "I can't make it today, but I'd love to reschedule." Starting small allows you to build your confidence in asserting your needs. It's also important to practice self-compassion throughout this process. If you feel guilty or uncomfortable when setting a boundary, acknowledge those feelings without judgment. Understand that it's okay to feel conflicted but that your well-being is important and worth protecting.

5. Communicate Your Boundaries Clearly And Respectfully

One of the most critical aspects of boundary-setting is communication. It's not enough to feel that a boundary is necessary; you must also express it clearly and respectfully to others. This doesn't mean you have to be harsh or rigid, but it does mean being honest about your limits. For instance, you might say, "I need some quiet time after work to recharge so that I won't be available for calls in the evenings," or "I'm feeling overwhelmed right now, and I need some space." Communicating your needs clearly and respectfully prevents misunderstandings and ensures that others know your boundaries.

6. Recognize That Boundaries Can Be Fluid

Boundaries are not set in stone; they can change depending on the situation or context. For example, what you need in one relationship might differ from what you need in another, and your boundaries may evolve. For neurodivergent individuals, sensory needs or social limits can shift based on energy levels, stress, or life circumstances. Being flexible and compassionate with yourself when boundaries need to change is crucial for maintaining balance.

7. Trust Yourself And Honor Your Needs

Setting boundaries without guilt requires trusting yourself and honoring your needs. You are the expert of your experience, and your feelings and limits are valid. Trust that when you set boundaries, you are doing so because it's in your best interest emotionally, mentally, and physically. Letting go of guilt involves accepting that your needs are valid and necessary to be your most authentic self.

Setting boundaries without guilt is a skill that takes practice and self-awareness. It's about learning to value yourself and your needs while also recognizing that your worth is not dependent on constantly meeting the needs of others. By embracing your neurodivergence and learning to set healthy boundaries, you can create relationships and environments that honor who you are and allow you to thrive.

Communication Tools That Work

Effective communication is crucial for building strong relationships, especially for neurodivergent individuals who may experience unique challenges in expressing themselves and understanding others. Whether you're dealing with ADHD, autism, or other neurodivergent traits, finding communication tools that work for you can make a huge difference in navigating both personal and professional interactions. This section will explore a few communication tools that can help neurodivergent individuals improve clarity, reduce misunderstandings, and foster more meaningful connections.

1. Direct And Clear Language

Direct and explicit language is one of the most effective tools for improving communication. Neurodivergent individuals, particularly those with autism or ADHD, may find it challenging to interpret vague or indirect communication. Therefore, it's helpful to be as specific as possible in speaking and writing. Instead of saying something ambiguous like, "Can you help me with that later?" try saying, "Can you help me with that at 3 PM today?" Being direct can prevent confusion, ensure everyone is on the same page, and help you communicate your needs without leaving room for misinterpretation.

Writing things down can be incredibly effective for individuals who struggle with expressing themselves verbally. Using written communication allows time to think through responses and organize thoughts in a way that may be more difficult in real-time conversations. It also gives others a chance to review what was said and respond thoughtfully, reducing the opportunity for misunderstandings.

2. **Visual Supports And Cues**

Visual supports are another helpful communication tool. Many neurodivergent individuals process information better when it's presented visually, whether through charts, diagrams, written instructions, or even pictures. Visual cues can serve as reminders, help with organizing thoughts, or illustrate instructions in a more digestible way.

For instance, a color-coded calendar or a visual checklist can help you organize tasks or manage your schedule without feeling overwhelmed by a sea of information. In social situations, visual cues like gestures or body language can help express emotions or intentions more clearly, especially for those who find verbalizing emotions difficult. In professional or social settings, it's also valuable to use visual aids when explaining complex ideas to ensure others understand your point of view.

3. **Active Listening Techniques**

Effective communication isn't just about how you express yourself it's also about how you listen to others. Active listening is an essential skill for any communicator.

Still, it can be particularly beneficial for neurodivergent individuals who sometimes struggle to focus or process information during conversations.

To practice active listening, give the speaker your full attention, avoid interrupting, and paraphrase what they've said to ensure you understand. This not only clarifies the conversation but also shows respect for the speaker's point of view. For people with ADHD, it might help to ask follow-up questions or take notes during conversations to stay engaged and retain information more effectively.

4. Self-Advocacy Tools

One of the most empowering communication tools is self-advocacy. Learning to advocate for your needs whether in a workplace setting, with family, or in social situations can improve communication and reduce stress. If you find it difficult to understand social cues or need extra time to process information, let others know that upfront. For example, you might say, "I process information slowly, so I may need a moment to respond," or "I need clear instructions to help me stay on track."

Explaining your communication preferences allows others to adjust and create a more supportive and understanding environment. Self-advocacy also includes expressing your boundaries clearly, such as requesting breaks during long meetings or needing space in social situations to avoid feeling overwhelmed.

5. **Digital Tools And Apps**

In today's digital age, numerous apps and tools can support communication, especially for neurodivergent individuals. For example, productivity apps like Trello or Todoist can help organize tasks visually and track essential deadlines. Note-taking apps like Notion or Evernote can help consolidate ideas and create clear action plans.

Speech-tc-text tools, such as Google Dictation or Otter.ai, can also help you express thoughts more easily without needing to type or write manually. Text-based platforms like email or messaging apps may be preferred for social communication, as they offer time to process and respond at your own pace.

6. **Therapy And Support Groups**

Finally, seeking support from therapy or support groups can offer valuable communication tools. Cognitive-behavioral therapy (CBT) and other therapeutic approaches can help individuals develop skills for better communication, emotional regulation, and conflict resolution. Support groups, whether in-person or online, can provide an opportunity to share experiences, learn from others, and develop communication strategies specific to your neurodivergent needs.

By using these communication tools, neurodivergent individuals can enhance their interactions with others, build stronger relationships, and reduce stress in personal and professional settings. Whether through direct language, visual supports, or self-advocacy, these tools empower you to communicate authentically and effectively, ensuring your voice is heard and understood.

Chapter 8

Work, Burnout & Capitalism

In today's fast-paced, productivity-driven world, the intersection of work, burnout, and capitalism can feel overwhelming especially for neurodivergent individuals. The demands of modern work environments, which often prioritize efficiency and conformity, can be draining for those who experience the world differently, particularly those with ADHD or autism. Neurodivergent individuals may struggle with sensory overload, time management, and executive function challenges, which can lead to higher rates of burnout.

Capitalism exacerbates these challenges by emphasizing continuous growth, profit, and individual success. The pressure to perform, meet deadlines, and constantly "do more" creates a system where rest and self-care are often considered luxuries, not necessities. In this context, burnout becomes a personal struggle and a systemic issue that broadly affects workers.

This chapter will explore how the capitalist work culture contributes to burnout, particularly for neurodivergent people. We will discuss the expectations placed on workers, the physical and emotional toll of constant productivity, and the importance of redefining success to prioritize well-being over profit. It's time to confront the realities of work culture and find ways to create sustainable, balanced lives amidst these pressures.

Adhd/Autistic Burnout Is Real (And Different From Regular Burnout)

Burnout is a term that has become widely recognized and is often used to describe the physical, emotional, and mental exhaustion people experience from excessive stress or overwork. However, for neurodivergent individuals, particularly those with ADHD or autism, burnout can take on a different, more complex form that goes beyond the typical exhaustion associated with regular burnout. ADHD and autistic burnout are not just about being tired—they are about reaching a point where the demands of the world overwhelm the coping mechanisms and internal resources that neurodivergent people rely on to function daily.

1. What Makes Adhd/Autistic Burnout Different?

While regular burnout is often linked to external stressors like work, family obligations, or societal expectations, ADHD and autistic burnout are more intimately tied to internal struggles and how neurodivergent individuals interact with the world around them. For someone with ADHD, burnout can be triggered by a prolonged period of difficulty managing executive function tasks like staying organized, meeting deadlines, and following through with commitments. These constant challenges can lead to a buildup of frustration, self-blame, and exhaustion.

For autistic individuals, burnout often occurs after extended periods of masking or suppressing their true selves in social situations. Autistic burnout can also result from sensory overload when the overwhelming amount of sensory stimuli (such as bright lights, loud sounds, or crowded environments) becomes too much to bear. This constant self-monitoring, alongside the struggle to meet social expectations, can leave autistic people feeling depleted, isolated, and unable to continue functioning.

2. **Symptoms Of Adhd/Autistic Burnout**

ADHD and autistic burnout can manifest in a variety of ways that are distinct from general burnout. While regular burnout may primarily result in fatigue, loss of motivation, and decreased productivity, neurodivergent burnout can include more intense symptoms. Common signs include:

- **Physical exhaustion**: The fatigue in neurodivergent burnout is often more profound than typical exhaustion. It's the kind of tiredness that a good night's sleep cannot alleviate. Even the thought of doing everyday tasks can feel overwhelming.

- **Emotional dysregulation**: For those with ADHD and autism, burnout can lead to heightened emotions like irritability, anxiety, and deep sadness because their usual coping mechanisms are no longer functioning effectively.

- **Sensory overload**: In autistic burnout, sensory stimuli become almost unbearable. Noises, lights, textures, and even certain smells can feel overwhelming and physically painful, making it difficult to leave the house or interact with others.

- **Social withdrawal**: People with ADHD and autism may retreat from social situations entirely during burnout. Interacting with others, which requires significant effort due to masking, becomes impossible. They may shut down or isolate themselves to avoid further overstimulation.

- **Cognitive difficulties**: Burnout in neurodivergent individuals often leads to significantly declining cognitive functions like memory, attention, and processing speed. Even basic tasks can become mentally exhausting or feel impossible to complete.

3. **Why Does Adhd/Autistic Burnout Happen?**

Neurodivergent burnout is primarily a result of prolonged stress, and the constant exertion required to navigate a world that isn't designed for people with ADHD or autism. For those with ADHD, the challenges of staying on top of tasks, managing time effectively, and maintaining focus can be emotionally and mentally taxing. For autistic individuals, the strain of constantly monitoring behavior, suppressing natural inclinations, and enduring sensory overload can create a tipping point where the body and mind shut down.

Both conditions involve significant cognitive and emotional effort to adapt to societal expectations, social norms, and daily tasks. Over time, this effort takes its toll, leading to burnout.

4. **Recovery From Adhd/Autistic Burnout**

Recovering from neurodivergent burnout requires more than just resting it requires a shift in how neurodivergent individuals engage with the world around them. While regular burnout may improve with some time off, ADHD and autistic burnout can require significant time for self-regulation, rest, and restructuring one's environment. Recovery can be a slow, deliberate process, and it often involves:

- **Rest**: Getting adequate sleep and taking breaks is essential, but for neurodivergent individuals, rest may also involve reducing social interactions, minimizing sensory overload, and creating a calm, quiet environment.

- **Reevaluating responsibilities**: Recovery often involves stepping back from work, social obligations, or other commitments that may be overwhelming. Setting boundaries and learning to say no can be a key part of healing.

- **Self-compassion**: For neurodivergent individuals, the experience of burnout can often be accompanied by feelings of guilt or shame. Acknowledging that it's okay to need time to recover and practicing self-compassion is an integral part of healing.

ADHD and autistic burnout are not just about being tired or overworked, they are about the overwhelming, cumulative effects of trying to survive in a world that doesn't accommodate the unique needs of neurodivergent individuals. Understanding that these types of burnout are real and different from regular burnout is crucial for both neurodivergent people and those around them. By acknowledging the specific challenges that come with ADHD and autism and allowing for recovery that takes those challenges into account, neurodivergent individuals can begin to heal, rebuild their energy, and regain their sense of self.

Navigating Neurotypical Workspaces

Navigating a neurotypical workspace can be especially challenging for neurodivergent individuals, including those with ADHD, autism, or other cognitive differences. Work environments are often designed with the neurotypical person in mind, meaning they may not accommodate the sensory, social, and mental needs of neurodivergent employees. From the expectations of social interactions to the pressure of constantly multitasking, neurodivergent individuals can find themselves at odds with a system that doesn't cater to their unique ways of working. However, navigating these spaces and thriving with the right tools and strategies is possible.

1. **Understanding The Challenges**

One of the biggest challenges for neurodivergent individuals in a neurotypical workspace is sensory overload. Bright lights, constant noise, or the feeling of being crowded can be overwhelming for those with sensory sensitivities, which is especially true for people on the autism spectrum. Similarly, employees with ADHD may struggle with focus and time management in a fast-paced environment that demands multitasking and constant shifts in attention.

Another challenge is navigating social norms and expectations. Neurodivergent individuals may find it difficult to pick up on subtle social cues, leading to misunderstandings or feelings of isolation. For example, individuals with autism might not always engage in small talk, or those with ADHD may struggle to stay on track during meetings. These differences can sometimes be misinterpreted by neurotypical colleagues, leading to frustration or exclusion.

2. **Strategies For Success**

- **Open Communication and Self-Advocacy**

Effective communication is one of the most essential tools for navigating a neurotypical workspace. Being open about your needs and challenges can help colleagues and managers understand how to support you best. If you have sensory sensitivities, request a quieter workspace or noise-canceling headphones. If you struggle with multitasking, discuss ways to break down tasks into manageable steps with clear deadlines.

• Structure and Routine

Creating structure and routine can mitigate challenges related to time management and staying organized. Use planners, apps, or digital reminders to keep up with tasks. Setting clear work hours and breaking your work into smaller, more manageable chunks can also make a big difference.

• Setting Boundaries

Setting clear boundaries is crucial for protecting your mental health in a neurotypical workspace. Don't hesitate to ask for quiet time or to take breaks when you feel overwhelmed. Let colleagues know if you need time to process information before responding or prefer written communication rather than verbal.

• Find Allies

Building relationships with understanding colleagues or managers can be incredibly helpful. Having an ally at work can provide security and help you navigate social and professional challenges. Allies can advocate for you, provide emotional support, and help you feel included.

While navigating a neurotypical workspace may feel challenging, it's possible to thrive with the right tools and strategies. By advocating for yourself, creating structure, setting boundaries, and finding allies, you can manage the demands of the workplace while honoring your neurodivergent needs. The key is recognizing that asking for what you need and creating an environment supporting your success is okay.

Designing A Work-Life That Honors Your Brain

For neurodivergent individuals, such as those with ADHD or autism, designing a work life that honors your brain is essential for maintaining productivity, mental well-being, and overall satisfaction. Traditional work environments often demand multitasking, rigid schedules, and social norms that may not align with how neurodivergent individuals think, process, or interact with the world. You can foster a healthier, more sustainable balance between work and well-being by intentionally crafting a work life that considers your brain's unique needs.

1. Understanding Your Strengths And Challenges

The first step in designing a work life that suits you is understanding your neurodivergent traits both strengths and challenges. People with ADHD, for example, may have high levels of creativity and problem-solving skills, but they might struggle with maintaining focus, organizing tasks, or managing time. Conversely, individuals on the autism spectrum may excel in detail-oriented tasks but face difficulties with social interactions or sensory sensitivities.

By identifying your strengths and challenges, you can seek work that aligns with your natural abilities and avoid tasks that play into areas where you're more likely to struggle. Designing your work life around tasks that maximize your strengths while minimizing stressors that exacerbate difficulties is essential.

2. Creating A Flexible Schedule

One key aspect of designing a work life that honors your brain is flexibility. For neurodivergent individuals, the typical 9-to-5 schedule may not be ideal. Flexible work hours allow you to work when your energy and focus peak. For those with ADHD, working in shorter bursts with frequent breaks can help maintain concentration without burning out. Similarly, those on the autism spectrum might need time to recharge after social interactions or sensory overload, and having control over your schedule can make a big difference.

Consider the environment in which you work. If you're sensitive to noise or bright lights, create a quiet workspace or use noise-canceling headphones to minimize distractions.

3. Setting Clear Boundaries And Expectations

Setting clear boundaries with colleagues and supervisors is essential to protect your mental health and avoid burnout. For instance, don't hesitate to ask for help or delegate if you find specific tasks overwhelming. Let your managers know if you need extra time to process information or if you prefer written communication over meetings.

Setting boundaries also means knowing when to say no. Avoid overloading yourself with too many tasks or social obligations. Learn to recognize when your brain is reaching its limit and let yourself step back when needed.

4. Using Tools And Systems To Stay Organized

Organization can be a significant challenge for neurodivergent individuals, particularly for those with ADHD. Implementing tools and systems can streamline daily tasks and reduce mental clutter. Digital tools like Trello, Asana, or Todoist can manage tasks visually, breaking down complex projects into smaller, more manageable steps. Setting reminders and using calendar apps can help you stay on track without feeling overwhelmed by deadlines.

For individuals on the autism spectrum, visual supports like charts, calendars, and flowcharts can effectively organize work and reduce anxiety about what needs to be done.

5. Prioritizing Self-Care

Finally, honoring your brain means prioritizing self-care. A healthy work-life balance is vital for avoiding burnout. Schedule regular breaks throughout the day, primarily if you work in an environment that demands intense focus. Whether it's a walk outside, practicing mindfulness, or engaging in a hobby, take time to reset and recharge. By regularly checking in with yourself and acknowledging when you need rest or support, you'll be better equipped to handle the demands of your work life without compromising your well-being.

Designing a work life that honors your brain requires consciously understanding your unique needs, strengths, and challenges. By prioritizing flexibility, setting clear boundaries, utilizing organizational tools, and ensuring proper self-care, neurodivergent individuals can create a work environment that supports both productivity and mental health. A work life that aligns with your neurodivergent brain leads to better outcomes and fosters a sense of fulfillment and authenticity.

Chapter 9

Daily Life: Routines, Chaos & Radical Acceptance

Navigating daily life as a neurodivergent individual often involves balancing the desire for structure and the inevitable chaos that can arise from executive function challenges, sensory overload, or social demands. For those with ADHD, autism, or other neurodivergent traits, the rhythm of daily life can feel unpredictable, sometimes chaotic, and often overwhelming. But rather than forcing yourself into a "perfect" routine or suppressing the natural ebb and flow of your days, embracing radical acceptance can be a powerful tool for finding peace and stability.

Radical acceptance is about acknowledging your experiences without judgment accepting that some days will feel more chaotic than others and that it's okay not to meet every expectation placed on you. It involves letting go of the guilt that often comes with struggling to maintain a perfectly structured routine and instead focusing on the small, manageable changes you can make to support your well-being.

This chapter will explore how to build routines that honor your neurodivergent needs while accepting life's unpredictable nature. It will discuss how radical acceptance can help reduce stress, foster self-compassion, and empower you to navigate your days with greater ease and less frustration.

Systems That Help (And Those That Don't)

When managing daily life as a neurodivergent individual, the right systems can make a difference. People with ADHD, autism, or other neurodivergent traits often face unique challenges when it comes to organization, time management, and routine. The right tools and strategies can support executive functioning, reduce stress, and improve overall quality of life. However, not all systems are created equal, and some can be more hindrance than help. Knowing which systems work for you and which don't can significantly ease your journey toward finding balance and efficiency.

1. **Systems That Help**

- **Visual Planning Tools**

For many neurodivergent individuals, visual systems are incredibly effective. Tools like calendars, charts, whiteboards, or digital apps with visual interfaces can make tracking tasks and staying organized easier. For example, apps like Trello or Notion allow you to create visual boards that break tasks into manageable chunks, making prioritizing and tracking progress easier. Using color coding or different symbols to categorize tasks can help clarify and reduce the mental load of remembering everything at once.

- **Time Management Aids**

Time blindness, or difficulty perceiving time accurately, is common for individuals with ADHD. To combat this, using timers, alarms, or time-blocking techniques can help create structure. The Pomodoro Technique, which involves working in short bursts with scheduled breaks, is beneficial for those with ADHD, as it encourages focus while preventing burnout. Digital tools like Focus Booster or Toggl also offer time-tracking systems to help maintain progress and accountability.

- **Routine and Habit Tracking**

Establishing consistent routines can be a game-changer for neurodivergent individuals. Using apps like Habitica or Streaks, which track daily tasks and goals, can make routine-building more enjoyable and motivating. These systems offer immediate feedback, reinforcing progress and creating a sense of accomplishment. Routine-building tools work exceptionally well for those with ADHD, helping them establish structure without overwhelming their minds.

- **Sensory Modulation Systems**

For those with autism or sensory sensitivities, creating systems that address sensory input can improve daily functioning. Noise-canceling headphones, soft lighting, or fidget tools can reduce overwhelm and increase focus. Environmental adjustments, such as minimizing clutter or creating sensory-friendly spaces, can significantly affect mental clarity and comfort.

2. Systems That Don't Help

• Overly Complex Organizational Systems

While the proper structure is essential, overly complicated organizational systems can quickly become a source of stress. Complex filing systems, intricate planners with too many steps, or trying to juggle multiple apps or tools can overwhelm the brain, leading to burnout. For individuals with ADHD, too many steps or excessive detail can be paralyzing, causing them to disengage entirely. The key is simplicity systems should streamline, not complicate, daily tasks.

• Rigid, One-Size-Fits-All Routines

While routines are essential, they shouldn't be so rigid that they feel suffocating or impossible to maintain. Neurodivergent individuals often struggle with the constant pressure of perfectionism, and a routine that doesn't allow for flexibility can contribute to stress and self-criticism. A "one-size-fits-all" approach, where systems demand constant adherence to an idealized structure, can feel like an unrealistic standard. Adapting systems that allow for flexibility based on changing needs and energy levels is essential.

- **Excessive Multitasking**

Multitasking can be a significant challenge for those with ADHD, as it often leads to a lack of focus and incomplete tasks. Systems that require or encourage multitasking such as constant email checking or juggling multiple tasks usually make things worse rather than better. It's better to implement systems that focus on single-tasking or limit distractions, such as using the "single-task focus" method or setting times for uninterrupted, deep work.

- **Over-Scheduling**

An over-scheduled day can lead to burnout, particularly for neurodivergent individuals who may already feel overstimulated or struggle with executive function. Systems that pack the calendar with back-to-back meetings, tasks, or activities can leave little room for the necessary breaks or downtime. Over-scheduling can also cause anxiety about meeting expectations, leading to avoidance or disengagement. Leaving time for rest and flexibility is crucial, leading to better productivity and mental well-being.

The right systems can serve as vital tools for neurodivergent individuals, but not all systems are equally effective. Visual tools, time management strategies, habit trackers, and sensory modulation systems are the most helpful, as they provide structure without overwhelming the individual. On the other hand, overly complex or rigid systems, excessive multitasking, and over-scheduling can create more problems than solutions, increasing stress and anxiety. Ultimately, the best systems can be personalized to fit your unique needs, offering simplicity, flexibility, and balance. Designing a system that honors your brain and accommodates your neurodivergent traits is key to creating a sustainable, productive, and fulfilling life.

Spoon Theory, Executive Dysfunction, And Surviving Monday

For many neurodivergent folks, just getting through a Monday can feel like climbing a mountain in flip-flops. It's not just "not liking Mondays" it's often a real and tangible drain on mental, emotional, and physical resources. Enter *spoon theory* and *executive dysfunction* two frameworks that help explain why things that seem "simple" for others can feel monumentally hard for people with ADHD, autism, and other neurodivergent conditions.

1. Spoon Theory: Measuring Invisible Energy

Spoon theory, created by Christine Miserandino, is a metaphor used to explain the limited energy reserves people with chronic illness or disability often experience. In this model, "spoons" represent units of energy. Neurotypical people might wake up with an unlimited supply of spoons, but if you're neurodivergent, you might start your day with only five or even two. Getting out of bed might cost one. Answering emails could take another. When lunch rolls around, you might be out of spoons entirely.

For many of us, this isn't just about physical tiredness it's cognitive and emotional. Social interactions, noise, unexpected changes, and bright lights can cost spoons. So when someone says, "Why are you tired? You haven't done *that* much," spoon theory gives you the language to explain: "I've done *more* than enough with what I had."

2. Executive Dysfunction: The Invisible Wall

Now layer in executive dysfunction the frustrating, invisible force field that keeps you from starting, organizing, or finishing tasks even when you *want* to. Executive functions are the brain's management skills: planning, prioritizing, remembering, initiating tasks, and regulating emotions. Even small tasks like brushing your teeth, making a phone call, or opening a work document can feel impossible when they're not working as expected.

On Mondays, executive dysfunction can hit especially hard. After a weekend with unstructured time (or recovery from burnout), shifting into "productive mode" can feel like your brain lags behind your to-do list. You may *know* what you must do but can't make your body start. Then comes the shame spiral "Why can't I just do this?" which only deepens the fog.

3. Surviving Monday With Self-Compassion And Strategy

The first step in surviving Mondays (or any high-demand day) is to accept that your brain works differently and that's okay. Build your day around your capacity instead of forcing yourself into unrealistic expectations.

Here are a few strategies that can help:

- **Budget Your Spoons**

Before you jump into the day, do a mental inventory: How many spoons do I realistically have? Prioritize what's necessary, and give yourself permission to delay or drop tasks that can wait. You're not lazy you're resourceful with your limited energy.

- **Micro-Tasks**

Break everything down. Instead of "clean the kitchen," try "pick up trash," "put away dishes," or "wipe one counter." Checking off small wins builds momentum and reduces overwhelm.

- **Use External Supports**

Timers, to-do lists, voice memos, and body-doubling (working alongside someone else) can be powerful tools for overcoming executive dysfunction. They take some cognitive load off your brain and help get you started.

- **Rest Without Guilt**

Do it if you need to lie down at noon on a Monday. Rest is not a reward; it's a requirement. Spoon conservation today means you'll have more for tomorrow.

- **Celebrate Small Victories**

Got out of bed? Brushed your teeth? Sent one email? That's progress. Honor it. Surviving a Monday with limited spoons and a brain that resists "productivity" is no small feat.

Spoon theory and executive dysfunction aren't excuses they're explanations. They help give language to the very real experiences of neurodivergent people navigating a world that wasn't designed with us in mind. So the next time you dread Monday, remember you're not alone, your energy is valid, and survival *is* an accomplishment.

Finding Your "Good Enough" Rhythm

One of the most liberating lessons for neurodivergent folks is realizing that "good enough" isn't a compromise it's a form of self-respect. In a world that constantly pushes perfection, productivity, and hustle culture, especially under capitalism, striving for an ideal routine or output can feel like trying to run a race with ankle weights. But when you start honoring your natural rhythms your energy cycles, attention span, sensory needs, and emotional states you begin to redefine success on your terms. Finding your "good enough" rhythm isn't about giving up. It's about shifting from self-judgment to self-trust.

1. Letting Go Of Perfectionism

Many neurodivergent adults, especially those diagnosed later in life, internalize the idea that they're always falling short. Whether it's messy rooms, missed deadlines, or "wasted" hours staring at the wall, these experiences can trigger a perfectionist spiral: If I can't do it right, why try?

But perfection is often the enemy of progress. "Good enough" means completing the task in a way that works for *you*, not necessarily how others would do it. It could mean doing your laundry but not folding it right away. Perhaps it could be answering emails in short, focused bursts rather than all at once progress, not perfection.

2. Recognizing Your Natural Patterns

Your energy and focus are not linear, and that's okay. Some days, you might be able to hyperfocus for hours, knocking out everything on your to-do list. Other days, brushing your teeth is the win of the day. Learning your natural rhythms when you feel most focused, when you crash and when you need to move or rest helps you design a routine that supports you instead of working against you.

Start tracking your patterns: What times of day are you most alert? When does your anxiety or sensory sensitivity peak? Over time, you can build your routine around those insights. Maybe your "good enough" morning involves music, no talking, and a slow start. That's not a flaw it's wisdom.

3. Building Flexibility Into Structure

Structure helps but only when it's flexible. Too rigid becomes another source of shame when you can't follow it perfectly. Too loose, and everything unravels. The sweet spot? Gentle scaffolding. Use tools like time blocking, habit trackers, or visual reminders, but leave room for change. If today's plan doesn't work, shift it. If a system starts to feel burdensome, adjust it.

"Good enough" structure adapts to your needs instead of forcing you to adjust.

4. **Celebrating Small Wins**

Acknowledging and celebrating small successes is key to reinforcing your "good enough" rhythm. Did you feed yourself? Take your meds? Cancel a plan because you needed rest? Those are all valid wins. You're not lazy caring for your brain in a world that often doesn't understand how much effort that takes.

Your "good enough" rhythm isn't about settling it's about living more honestly and gently with yourself. It's where grace meets growth. When you let go of unrealistic standards and embrace what works for *you*, life becomes less about catching up and more about showing up. And that, in itself, is more than enough.

Chapter 10

Intersectionality, Oppression & Neurodivergent Rage

L iving at the intersection of neurodivergence and marginalized identities whether through race, gender, sexuality, disability, or class means navigating a world layered with compounding forms of oppression. It's not just that the systems weren't built for us; they actively exclude, silence, and harm us. For neurodivergent people who are also BIPOC, women, queer, or otherwise marginalized, daily life often feels like walking through a maze of microaggressions, invalidation, erasure, and systemic barriers.

And beneath that constant pressure? Rage. Not the kind of rage born from entitlement but the deep, simmering fury that comes from being misunderstood, overlooked, or punished for existing authentically. Neurodivergent rage is sacred the fire that burnt through the lies we've been told about ourselves. It's the energy that arises when we finally realize we were never broken, just buried.

This chapter dives into that righteous anger not to glorify pain but to name it, hold space for it, and channel it. When we understand how oppression has shaped our neurodivergent experience, we begin to reclaim our power. Intersectionality gives us the language. Rage gives us the fuel. Together, they carve the path to liberation.

Living At The Crossroads Of Race, Gender, And Neurodivergence

To live at the intersection of race, gender, and neurodivergence is to constantly navigate a world that was not built with you in mind. Each identity on its own can shape how you experience the world. But when they overlap, the complexity and weight of existing in society can intensify in ways that are hard to explain to those who haven't lived it.

For BIPOC individuals, systemic racism is already a daily hurdle. Add gender marginalization, being a woman, nonbinary, or gender-expansive, and the societal expectations multiply. Now fold in neurodivergence, and you get a life lived in layers of masking, code-switching, people-pleasing, shrinking, and overperforming just to be seen as enough. These overlapping identities create a unique form of erasure. Neurodivergence is still primarily associated with white, cisgender boys, and that narrow lens has left countless BIPOC and gender-diverse individuals undiagnosed, misdiagnosed, or dismissed.

Many of us learn how to camouflage to survive from an early age. We are told we are "too much" or "not enough." We are too loud, too quiet, too sensitive, too intense, or too scattered. We are praised when we comply and punished when we deviate. The pressure to conform is relentless, and often, we internalize the idea that our struggles are moral failings, not symptoms of an unrecognized neurodivergent brain in a world hostile to difference.

Healthcare providers, educators, and even mental health professionals often carry implicit biases that shape their expectations of what ADHD or autism looks like. When you're a Black girl who zones out in class, it's seen as defiance, not inattentiveness. When you're a Latina struggling with sensory overload, it's being dramatic. When you're an Asian femme masking your way through life, your suffering is overlooked because you seem high achieving. The intersection of race and gender filters how our behaviors are perceived and misperceived.

And then there's the exhaustion the exhaustion of constantly translating yourself, of wondering if your stimming, your social confusion, your burnout will be read as unprofessional, unstable, or unworthy, of knowing that being weird can carry real consequences depending on how the world sees your body and your identity. But there's also power in this crossroads.

When you've lived on the margins, you develop a cultural fluency and emotional intelligence that neurotypical spaces often lack. You know how to read a room, code switch on a dime, and translate your needs in three different ways. You know how to survive systems never designed for you and still find ways to thrive. That resilience isn't accidental. It's hard-earned.

The intersection of race, gender, and neurodivergence illuminates where the world has failed us and highlights the unique ways we adapt, resist, and reimagine. We don't just live at this crossroads; we build from it. We create new language, new pathways, and new blueprints for what neurodivergent life can look like when we center our full, complex selves. Not broken. Not too much. Just whole and finally seen.

"Strong Black Woman" & "Model Minority" Traps

For many neurodivergent people of color, the journey toward self-understanding is tangled in cultural expectations and survival narratives that were never designed to hold our complexity. Two of the most insidious and deeply rooted traps are the "Strong Black Woman" trope and the "Model Minority" myth. Though they may seem like compliments on the surface strength, resilience, intelligence they often serve as cages that silence struggle, invalidate pain, and delay diagnosis.

The "Strong Black Woman" trope demands that Black women be unbreakable, endlessly nurturing, and emotionally bulletproof. This stereotype doesn't allow room for softness, rest, or vulnerability let alone neurodivergent traits like emotional dysregulation, executive dysfunction, or sensory overwhelm. When a Black woman expresses fatigue, confusion, or mental health concerns, she's often dismissed. She's expected to keep pushing, holding everyone else together, and proving her worth just to be seen as "doing okay." The pressure to carry everything gracefully makes asking for help feel like a failure. And when a late ADHD or autism diagnosis finally arrives, the grief isn't just about missed signs—it's about all the years you had to be superhuman to survive.

Meanwhile, the "Model Minority" myth, often applied to Asian communities, paints a picture of quiet, academically gifted, obedient individuals who don't make trouble. This myth flattens entire cultures and erases the struggles of those who don't or can't conform to that image. For neurodivergent Asians, especially women, and femmes, this narrative is stifling. It encourages masking from an early age, discourages open conversations about mental health, and treats achievement as proof of well-being.

Your struggles must not be real if you succeed in school or work. If you're overwhelmed, it must be a personal weakness, not a sign of an unseen condition. It becomes nearly impossible to advocate for yourself without feeling like you're disappointing your family or community.

Both traps are rooted in white supremacy. They were created to control how marginalized people move through the world rewarding silence, obedience, and self-sacrifice while punishing deviation. And both actively harm neurodivergent folks by making our challenges invisible and our needs inconvenient.

Nicci Brochard & Dr. Ben Chuba

These myths are especially dangerous because they force many of us into chronic over functioning. We learn to push through burnout, suppress our discomfort, and internalize that our value is tied to performance. The result? Diagnoses come late, if at all. Help is delayed. Self-worth becomes conditional. And all the while, we're suffering silently behind the masks we were told we had to wear.

Breaking free from these traps means reclaiming our humanity. It means allowing ourselves to be complex, contradictory, and in need. It means redefining strength not as silence or stoicism, but as the courage to rest, feel, and ask for support. We are allowed to be more than what the world expects of us. We are allowed to be whole. We can be neurodivergent in ways that challenge myths and rewrite stories.

Transforming Rage Into Resistance And Healing

Rage is not the enemy. For neurodivergent people, especially those from marginalized communities, rage is often one of the first honest emotions we feel after years of silence, gaslighting, and internalized shame. When we finally begin to uncover who we are beyond the masks, beyond the myths the rage can be overwhelming. But it's also powerful. This chapter is about honoring that fire and learning how to transform it into resistance and healing.

1. Understanding Where The Rage Comes From

Neurodivergent rage isn't just about missed diagnoses or unfair treatment. It's about decades of being told we were wrong for existing the way we do. It's the pain of being punished for symptoms we didn't understand. It's the heartbreak of realizing that life could've been so different if someone had just *seen us* earlier.

It's the rage of being underestimated, dismissed, overburdened, and overlooked. And for BIPOC and women, it's layered with systemic racism, sexism, and the pressure to overperform to be considered *barely enough*. This rage is righteous and naming its sources is the first step to transforming it.

2. Permitting Yourself To Feel It

So many of us have been taught that anger is dangerous or shameful, especially if we're socialized as women or raised in cultures that prize obedience and emotional restraint. But suppressing anger doesn't make it disappear it festers. It turns inward, morphing into depression, anxiety, self-doubt, or chronic burnout.

Allow yourself to feel your rage without an apology. Scream into a pillow. Write it all down in raw, messy words. Cry. Punch a cushion. Shake. Move your body. Your emotions are valid, and you don't owe anyone politeness while processing pain. Rage doesn't make you broken. It means you're finally telling the truth.

3. **Rage As A Signal And A Guide**

Anger is not just a reaction it's information. It tells you what matters. What's been violated? What boundaries were crossed? What you never received but desperately needed. When you listen to your rage, it becomes a guide toward the life you deserve.

Instead of asking, "Why am I so angry?" ask, "What is this anger trying to protect?" Often, it's the part of you that never felt safe, the part that needed to be heard, the part that deserved better.

Your rage can clarify your values, spotlight injustice, and fuel change not just internally but in your community and beyond.

4. **Channeling Rage Into Resistance**

Resistance is more than protest; it's a daily act of choosing yourself in a world that profits off your silence. When you speak up for your needs, stop masking, set boundaries, and share your truth, you are resisting. You are breaking generational patterns and systemic narratives that told you to stay small and quiet.

Transforming rage into resistance means creating from that fire. Write your story. Start a support group. Organize for better access in your workplace. Educate others about neurodivergence. Advocate for people like you who are still waiting to be seen.

Rage becomes resistant when you choose to build instead of burn out. When you shift from reaction to action, you reclaim your power.

5. **Letting Healing In**

Rage cracks us open, but healing fills the spaces with truth, softness, and strength. Healing doesn't mean you stop being angry. It implies that anger no longer controls you. It's just one part of your story, not the whole book.

Healing happens when you build a life where your needs are met and centered, surround yourself with people who *get it*, speak to yourself with compassion instead of critique, rest without guilt, and stop performing and start living as your whole, messy, radiant self.

Sometimes, healing looks like fire. Sometimes, it seems like stillness. Both are valid and necessary.

6. **Creating Space For Others On The Journey**

As you move through your transformation, remember your story is a light for others. The more we normalize neurodivergent rage and healing, the more we create space for others to do the same. You're not alone. And you're not responsible for fixing the whole world but you *can* be part of the shift.

Speak up when you can, hold space when you can, and be gentle when you cannot. Community is how we rise. And when our rage meets our love, real liberation begins.

Rage is a sacred part of the neurodivergent experience, especially for those who have lived too long in the shadows of systems that never saw us. But you are not too angry. You are not too much. You are just beginning to fully feel and that's where everything starts to change. Rage, when honored, can be the bridge to resistance and the soil for your healing. You don't need to "calm down." You need to rise with fire, clarity, and grace.

Chapter 11

Humor As A Healing Tool

When life hands you late diagnoses, misunderstood meltdowns, sensory overloads at family functions, and years of internalized shame, humor might seem like the last thing you'd reach for. But for many neurodivergent folks especially those navigating multiple marginalized identities humor is not just a coping mechanism. It's a survival strategy. A pressure valve. It is a way to reclaim power in the face of absurdity, injustice, and constant "You don't look autistic" microaggressions.

Humor allows us to name our truth without apology. It turns chaos into punchlines and helps us process pain without getting swallowed. The inside joke makes us feel seen, the sarcastic meme that breaks the tension, the belly laugh that cracks through burnout. For BIPOC, women, and other often-overlooked neurodivergent folks, humor can be both resistance and refuge.

This chapter explores how laughter, wit, and even dark humor can offer radical healing. Not because the struggles aren't real but because sometimes, laughing *with* yourself is the most revolutionary thing you can do. We're not broken, we're hilarious. And sometimes, the best way to say, "I'm still here" is with a smirk, a side-eye, and a story that makes the whole room say, "Wait… same."

Laughing At The Chaos (Without Minimizing It)

Neurodivergent life is messy. Routines fall apart. You forget the thing you were holding. You walk into a room and immediately forget why. Your brain decides 2 AM is the perfect time to reorganize the spice rack, and you've cried in the frozen food aisle more than once. There's chaos, big and small, and sometimes the only sane response is to laugh. Not because it's not hard. But, because laughter is often the first breath of relief in a world that demands too much and gives too little.

For those of us navigating ADHD, autism, or both, especially as BIPOC or women, we've been conditioned to take our struggles seriously. We've been taught to hustle harder, mask more, and quiet our breakdowns. So when we finally start naming the chaos, we might worry that laughing about it means we're not honoring how real the pain is. But humor and honesty can live side by side. Laughing at the absurdity doesn't mean denying the difficulty; it means reclaiming our narrative from shame.

There's power in saying, "Yeah, I just spent an hour looking for my glasses, which were on my face. Again." There's power in turning a sensory meltdown into a story with a punchline instead of just another moment you beat yourself up over. There's healing in those group chats full of memes that perfectly describe the mental gymnastics it takes to reply to an email. Neurodivergent humor isn't about making light of our struggles. It's about creating shared language around them, seeing ourselves in one another, and gently poking holes in the pressure always to have it together.

Sometimes, the chaos is so constant it starts to feel like character failure. You forget appointments, miss deadlines, get overwhelmed by simple tasks, and the self-judgment piles up fast. But it disrupts internalized shame when we can step back and laugh, even just a little. It gives us a moment of grace. It says, "Okay, yeah, that was ridiculous… but I'm still here." Humor helps us separate our identity from our symptoms. You are not a disaster; you live in a neurotypical world with a beautifully nonlinear brain.

And let's be real, some of the stuff we go through is genuinely funny in a surreal, "Did that just happen?" way. It's like when you hyperfocus for six hours and forget to eat, then get mad at yourself for being hungry. Or when you had a full-blown existential crisis over picking a toothpaste brand. Or when you were masking so hard, you forgot how you feel about something. These moments are frustrating, yes, but they're also uniquely ours. When we laugh at them, we're not making ourselves the joke; we refuse to let the chaos define us.

Of course, not all moments are laughable in the moment. And not everything should be turned into a joke. There's a difference between using humor as a healing tool and using it to dismiss your needs. It's okay to say, "This hurt," or "I need support." Humor should feel like a release, not a mask. If the laughter starts to feel forced or self-deprecating in a painful way, that's your cue to slow down and check in with yourself. Are you laughing to connect or to avoid?

The key is intentionality. Laugh at the chaos with yourself, not at yourself. Share the stories that make others feel less alone. Post the meme, write the tweet, and send the voice note that starts with "Okay, this is wild, but..." Let humor be a way to find your people, soften the edges of hard days, and remind yourself that even in a mess, there is joy. There is absurdity. There is you, resilient, real, and still laughing.

In the end, chaos will always be part of our neurodivergent journey. But if we can meet it with humor, honesty, and a wink at its ridiculousness, we take some of its power away. We remember that we're more than the mess. We're the meaning-makers. We're the chaos comedians. The ones who can drop a punchline in the middle of a meltdown and still make space for healing. And that is a kind of brilliance no system can define.

Neurodivergent Quirks That Are Awesome

Neurodivergence is often portrayed as requiring "fixing" or "correcting." However, if we take a step back, we'll see that many of the traits associated with ADHD, autism, and other neurodivergent experiences aren't just challenges they're superpowers. The quirks that make us different can also make us incredibly resilient, creative, and innovative. Below are some neurodivergent quirks that are pretty awesome.

1. Hyperfocus: The Superpower Of Getting Things Done

While many people struggle with maintaining attention, those of us with ADHD or autism can experience something called hyperfocus. This is when you become so engrossed in a task that everything else disappears. While it can be a double-edged sword (because it can be hard to pull away), it allows neurodivergent individuals to achieve incredible things when fully immersed in something they care about. Whether writing a novel, crafting a beautiful piece of art, or solving a complex problem, hyperfocus enables deep, uninterrupted concentration that leads to impressive accomplishments.

Instead of viewing hyperfocus as a problem, consider it a powerful tool. It helps us create, innovate, and produce with an intensity and passion many neurotypical people can only dream of.

2. **Exceptional Pattern Recognition: Seeing Connections Others**

Many neurodivergent people have an uncanny ability to recognize patterns. Whether through numbers, behavior, or complex systems, our brains are naturally wired to see connections others might overlook. This trait is prevalent in people with autism, where we may notice tiny details or inconsistencies that others miss.

This can be a significant strength in science, engineering, mathematics, and problem-solving. Our ability to identify patterns allows us to make unique contributions and even find creative solutions to longstanding issues. Our ability to zoom in and analyze can be the key to breakthroughs in a world that often overlooks minor details.

3. **Deep Empathy And Emotional Sensitivity: Feeling The World Around Us**

While neurodivergent individuals are often portrayed as lacking emotional understanding, the reality is quite the opposite. Many of us, especially those on the autism spectrum, experience emotions more intensely than others. This deep emotional sensitivity allows us to empathize with others on a level that can be profound. We feel what others feel, sometimes more than they do.

While this can be overwhelming, it can make us exceptional friends, partners, and allies. Our heightened sensitivity allows us to tune into the needs and emotions of those around us, offering compassion and understanding that may go unnoticed by others. Empathy is a rare and beautiful gift in a world that often feels emotionally disconnected.

4. Strong Sense Of Justice: A Passion For Fairness

Many neurodivergent people, especially those with autism, have a deeply ingrained sense of fairness. This often manifests as an unwavering commitment to justice, equality, and doing what's right. We are sensitive to hypocrisy, inequity, and unfair treatment. When we witness injustice, we are more likely to take action or speak out, even when it's uncomfortable.

This sense of justice is one of the reasons many neurodivergent individuals are drawn to activism or social causes. Our desire to create a fair and equal world drives us to challenge systems of oppression and fight for change, even when the odds are stacked against us.

5. Creativity And Out-Of-The-Box Thinking: The Art Of Innovation

Neurodivergence often comes with an incredible creative streak. Whether through art, writing, music, or problem-solving, many of us have a unique way of thinking that allows us to approach challenges from unexpected angles. While our brains may not always follow the conventional paths others take, they often lead us to innovative, groundbreaking ideas.

This out-of-the-box thinking can be transformative in creative industries and beyond. From new technological innovations to revolutionary art forms, neurodivergent minds have been responsible for some of the most groundbreaking ideas in history. We may not always fit into traditional structures, but that's where the magic happens by thinking differently, we create new possibilities.

6. Ability To See The Big Picture: Connecting Dots Across Domains

While some neurotypical individuals might focus on a single task or project, neurodivergent people often can connect seemingly unrelated dots. This means we can see the bigger picture how different ideas, concepts, or issues might intersect unexpectedly. We're not just looking at one thing but many things simultaneously, giving us a unique advantage in strategic planning, brainstorming, and innovation.

This ability is widespread in ADHD, where we can rapidly switch between tasks and see how they fit together. While it may appear like we're jumping from one thing to another, we are making connections that others might take years to recognize. Our multi-faceted perspective is a hidden strength that drives growth and change.

7. Unwavering Authenticity: No Pretending Necessary

One of the most beautiful aspects of neurodivergence is the ability to be unapologetically ourselves. Many neurodivergent people, particularly those on the autism spectrum, are known for their authenticity. We don't conform to social norms or try to fit in to please others. We say what we mean and act in ways that reflect who we truly are without masks or pretenses.

While this can be uncomfortable for some in a world that values conformity, it's also a remarkable trait. We are true to ourselves, regardless of societal expectations. Our authenticity fosters deeper connections and helps create spaces where others can feel safe to be themselves. We are the trailblazers for a world where individuality is celebrated, not hidden.

The quirks that come with being neurodivergent are not flaws to be fixed they are the unique traits that make us who we are. From hyperfocus to exceptional empathy, pattern recognition to creativity, these neurodivergent superpowers are not only beneficial to us but also to the world around us. By embracing these quirks, we can live fuller, richer lives and contribute to a society that values diverse ways of thinking and being. Our differences are not something to hide or apologize for they are the strengths that will help us change the world.

Building Joy Into Your Life On Purpose

In a world that often feels overwhelming, chaotic, or downright exhausting, joy can sometimes seem like an elusive luxury, a fleeting emotion we can only hope to experience on rare occasions. For neurodivergent individuals especially those with ADHD or autism joy may feel even more out of reach as daily life brings its own set of challenges and complexities. However, the truth is that pleasure does not happen to us by accident. We can intentionally create and nurture it, even in the midst of struggles, by building it into our lives on purpose.

Building joy isn't about forcing happiness or pretending everything is fine when it's not. It's about recognizing the little things that bring us joy, consciously making room for them in our busy lives, and actively cultivating an environment where joy can thrive. Here's how you can build joy into your life on purpose.

1. **Recognize The Things That Spark Joy**

The first step in building joy is recognizing what brings you joy. For neurodivergent individuals, these might not always be the same things that bring joy to others. What sparks joy for you might be quiet moments of solitude, a favorite hobby, sensory experiences, or even just watching the rain from your window. These things might seem small or insignificant to others, but they can be profound sources of joy if you make space for them.

Take time to notice the things that make you feel lighter, more content, or more at peace. It could be a song that lifts your spirits, a favorite cup of tea, or reading a book that transports you to another world. Start to make a list of these small joys, and don't be afraid to indulge in them. The more you acknowledge what brings you happiness, the easier it becomes to build them into your day-to-day routine intentionally.

2. **Prioritize Play And Creativity**

For many neurodivergent individuals, creative expression is a vital source of joy. Engaging in creative activities, whether painting, writing, cooking, or playing an instrument, can be incredibly fulfilling. But in the hustle of everyday life, it's easy to let creative pursuits fall by the wayside. We may feel there's no time for them, or they're not "productive" enough.

Play and creativity are essential to our mental and emotional well-being. They offer us a chance to express ourselves freely, without judgment or restriction. To build joy into your life, make time for play without the pressure to be perfect or produce something impressive. Allow yourself to doodle, sing, experiment in the kitchen, or dance around the living room. These moments of creative expression can reignite the spark of joy and remind you of the importance of playfulness in life.

3. Cultivate Mindfulness And Presence

Building joy is not always about doing more; sometimes, it's about being more present. Mindfulness whether through meditation, deep breathing, or simply paying attention to the present moment can help you tap into a more profound sense of peace and joy. Neurodivergent individuals may find that mindfulness practices help to calm the overwhelm that often comes with sensory overload or racing thoughts.

We can appreciate life more deeply when we're fully present in the moment. Instead of rushing from one task to the next or getting stuck in our heads, we allow ourselves to be present for the simple joys in life the warmth of the sun on our skin, the laughter of a friend, or the smell of a freshly brewed cup of coffee. Mindfulness doesn't have to be formal; it can simply be a conscious effort to engage with the world around you with intention and appreciation.

4. **Create Meaningful Connections**

As much as joy is an internal experience, it's also deeply connected to our relationships with others. For neurodivergent individuals, forming and maintaining connections can be challenging due to social differences, misunderstandings, or feeling out of sync with neurotypical expectations. However, joy naturally follows when we find people who genuinely understand and accept us.

Focus on creating meaningful connections with people who uplift you. Surround yourself with those who respect your boundaries, honor your neurodivergent traits, and share in your passions. Whether it's a close-knit circle of friends, a supportive partner, or a community that values your unique perspective, relationships built on mutual respect and understanding can be a powerful source of joy.

5. **Simplify Your Environment**

Clutter and chaos can dampen joy, especially for neurodivergent individuals who may experience sensory overload or executive dysfunction. Creating a calming, organized environment can make a difference in how you experience your day-to-day life. Whether decluttering your living space, creating designated areas for relaxation, or incorporating sensory-friendly elements like soft lighting or calming scents, an environment that nurtures peace can also nurture joy.

Take small steps to simplify your surroundings. Create zones for different activities work, relaxation, creativity so each space feels aligned with its purpose. Remove distractions and things that contribute to anxiety or stress, and instead, fill your space with things that spark happiness, like plants, art, or objects that remind you of happy memories. Your environment plays a significant role in shaping your mental and emotional state, so set it up in a way that promotes joy.

6. **Allow Yourself To Rest**

Rest is often overlooked or undervalued in a world that usually equates productivity with self-worth. However, true joy cannot be built without rest. For neurodivergent individuals, burnout can hit hard, especially when we constantly push ourselves to keep up with expectations that don't align with our needs. Allowing yourself to rest without guilt can actually help you recharge and find the joy that gets buried under exhaustion.

This means permitting yourself to slow down, say no to commitments that drain you, and take breaks when needed. Rest is not laziness. It's essential to maintaining your well-being and keeping your joy intact. Whether taking a nap, reading a book for pleasure, or simply doing nothing, rest is a key ingredient in building joy in your life.

Joy doesn't have to be a rare or fleeting experience. By intentionally creating space for the things that bring us happiness, we can actively build joy into our lives. For neurodivergent individuals, this process may look different, but it's no less important. Whether through recognizing small moments of happiness, prioritizing creativity, simplifying our environment, or embracing rest, we can cultivate joy every day. It's a practice, a choice, and a reminder that even in the chaos of life, we can find moments of peace, play, and purpose.

Chapter 12

Thriving Forward: Your Neurodivergent Future

T hriving Forward: Your Neurodivergent Future" is an invitation to embrace the unique strengths and challenges that come with neurodivergence, and to step confidently into a future filled with possibility. Whether you are navigating ADHD, autism, or other neurodivergent traits, this journey is about redefining what success and happiness look like for you. It's not about fitting into a world designed for others but creating a life that honors your brain's needs, passions, and potential.

This section explores how you can cultivate a future that isn't just about surviving but truly thriving. From practical strategies to emotional resilience, we'll focus on how to break free from limiting beliefs and societal expectations. It's about embracing who you are

Building Community And Finding Your People

For many neurodivergent individuals, one of the most potent sources of support and strength comes from the people around them. Building a community of like-minded individuals who understand, respect, and celebrate your neurodivergence can be a game-changer in how you navigate the world. Finding your people is about companionship and forging meaningful, authentic connections that foster mutual understanding and growth.

The journey to building a community can be complicated, especially for neurodivergent individuals who may feel disconnected from others due to differences in communication, interests, or social expectations. Social interactions can sometimes feel overwhelming or exhausting, and the pressure to fit into neurotypical spaces may lead to a sense of isolation. This is where intentionally finding a community that supports your neurodivergent identity can make all the difference.

1. **Embrace Online Communities**

One of the most accessible and valuable resources for finding your people is online communities. Whether on social media platforms, dedicated forums, or specialized websites, there are many spaces where neurodivergent individuals can connect. These online spaces often provide a sense of belonging and an opportunity to share experiences, advice, and insights with others who truly understand the unique challenges of being neurodivergent.

Social media platforms like Twitter, Instagram, and Reddit host vibrant neurodivergent communities that discuss daily struggles and personal triumphs. These platforms can help you find people who understand your experience and celebrate it. Joining these communities can help you feel less alone and more empowered as you connect with others who share similar experiences.

2. Seek Out Support Groups And Advocacy Organizations

Another valuable way to build community is by seeking out local or virtual support groups and advocacy organizations dedicated to neurodivergent individuals. These groups often provide a safe, supportive space to discuss challenges and share resources. They may offer opportunities for socializing, workshops, and advocacy, giving you a platform to share your voice while connecting with others who understand what it means to navigate the world as a neurodivergent individual.

Organizations that focus on ADHD, autism, or other neurodivergent conditions often hold events or create spaces for individuals to come together. These groups can help you develop deeper connections with others who are seeking belonging and understanding.

3. Prioritize Authentic Connections

When building a community, it's important to focus on finding authentic and reciprocal relationships. The goal isn't just to be surrounded by people but to be surrounded by people who lift you up and respect your individuality.

Nicci Brochard & Dr. Ben Chuba

Building these meaningful connections often involves seeking out people who value you for who you are rather than expecting you to conform to social norms that might not align with your neurodivergence.

Authentic connections can be made through shared interests, such as hobbies or passions, which align with your neurodivergent traits. For example, if you thrive on routine and find joy in structured activities, you may connect with others who share that preference. Similarly, suppose you enjoy sensory experiences or need time to recharge in solitude. In that case, some people understand that these preferences aren't just quirks but essential aspects of who you are.

4. **Embrace Diversity Within Neurodivergence**

Building a community isn't just about finding people similar to you in every way. Neurodivergent communities are rich in diversity, and connecting with individuals who may have different experiences from your own can be incredibly enriching. By embracing the diversity within neurodivergence whether in terms of gender, race, background, or neurotype you create opportunities for learning, growth, and solidarity.

For example, someone with ADHD might have different experiences navigating the world compared to someone with autism. Still, both individuals may share similar struggles related to sensory overload, executive dysfunction, or social challenges. Building a community where these differences are celebrated and respected allows a more holistic understanding of neurodivergence.

5. Take It Slow And Set Boundaries

Building a community takes time, and it's essential to recognize that relationships, like any other part of life, require effort and patience. It's okay to take things slow and set boundaries as you explore new connections. Boundaries are essential for maintaining healthy relationships. Being open about your needs whether it's a preference for structured communication or a need for time alone can help you build sustainable and fulfilling connections.

In some cases, it may take time to find your people. Not every connection will be a perfect fit, and that's okay. Trusting the process and knowing that your community is out there is essential. The key is to be open to the possibility of finding people who will appreciate you for who you are, not just who they think you should be.

Building a community as a neurodivergent individual isn't about fitting into any mold or adhering to societal expectations. It's about finding and creating a space where you can be authentic, surrounded by people who understand your experiences and support your growth. Whether through online communities, support groups, or personal connections, the right people can help you thrive. And, just as importantly, they'll remind you that you're not alone on your neurodivergent journey. So take the time to seek out your community, cultivate meaningful relationships, and allow yourself to be supported and celebrated. Your people are out there, waiting to connect with you.

What Healing Looks Like

Healing is not a linear process; it certainly doesn't look the same for everyone. For neurodivergent individuals, healing can be a profoundly personal journey of acceptance, self-discovery, and growth. It's important to understand that healing isn't about "fixing" what's broken but about embracing and nurturing every part of yourself, including your struggles.

Healing may begin with self-awareness understanding your neurodivergent traits and how they influence your life. This can be empowering, as it helps you reframe challenges as part of who you are, not something that needs to be erased. With this understanding, you can begin to cultivate self-compassion. This is essential, as it allows you to recognize that it's okay not to be perfect. You're allowed to make mistakes, experience setbacks, and feel frustrated. Healing is about showing yourself kindness in those moments.

For many, healing also involves unlearning harmful narratives and societal expectations that have shaped their self-perception. These might include the pressures to conform to neurotypical standards or the constant feeling of inadequacy due to not meeting external expectations. Healing is about reclaiming your power by redefining success on your terms, focusing on your strengths, and embracing your individuality.

Emotionally, healing often means accepting past experiences of misunderstanding, rejection, or misdiagnosis. It's a journey of grieving what could have been but also celebrating the new opportunities and perspectives that come with understanding your neurodivergence. There's often a mix of validation and grief a sense of relief that comes with the realization that you were never "lazy" or "broken," followed by sadness about missed opportunities or unacknowledged struggles.

Healing is also about building the resilience to face the future with confidence. It's not about being "cured" but about learning to navigate the world in ways that work for you. This might involve creating a life that fits your neurodivergent needs, whether adjusting your work environment, learning new coping strategies, or advocating for yourself in relationships.

Healing is about accepting yourself fully both the challenges and the strengths and finding peace with your journey. It's not a destination but an ongoing self-love, acceptance, and growth process.

A Final Love Letter To Your Past And Future Self

A final love letter to your past and future self is a beautiful act of reconciliation, acknowledgment, and hope. It's a chance to honor where you've been, accept what you've gone through, and celebrate how far you've come while embracing the possibilities ahead.

To my past self:

I see you. I see all the moments of confusion, frustration, and isolation that you felt, and I want you to know you were never truly alone, even when it seemed that way. You were doing the best you could with the tools and knowledge you had at the time. Those times when you questioned yourself wondering why things were so hard, why you didn't fit in, or why it always felt like something was missing those feelings were valid, even if you couldn't name them then.

You weren't "lazy" or "broken." You were neurodivergent in a world that didn't understand you, yet you kept going. You kept pushing forward, even when it was difficult. Though it felt like a weight at times, your resilience was your superpower. You survived. You learned. You grew.

And now, from this place of understanding, I want to thank you for holding on. Every experience, every tear, every moment of doubt it all brought you to this place of strength. I wish I could have told you then that you were perfect as you were and didn't have to fight so hard to fit into a world that wasn't designed for you. But here we are now, and I want you to know that you did a fantastic job, and I am proud of you. You are worthy of love and acceptance precisely as you are.

To my future self:

I am writing this with hope, anticipation, and trust in your journey. As you continue to evolve, I want you to remember that you don't have to be perfect. You don't have to meet anyone else's expectations of who you should be. What matters most is staying true to yourself, embracing your neurodivergent identity, and continuing to walk forward with confidence, knowing that your path is uniquely yours.

There will be times when the road ahead seems unclear, when you doubt yourself or face new challenges, but I want you to know that you can handle whatever comes your way. You have the strength, resilience, and wisdom that you've cultivated through the years. Remember to pause and be gentle with yourself when the world feels overwhelming. Healing isn't a race. It's okay to rest, to take breaks, and to do things at your own pace.

As you look to the future, I want you to celebrate every small victory, every moment of joy, and every step forward, no matter how small. Don't be afraid to dream big; don't let anyone tell you your dreams are impossible. Your journey is full of potential, possibility, and beauty.

Remember to surround yourself with people who see you, honor your uniqueness, and love you for who you truly are. Let those relationships nourish you, and don't be afraid to distance yourself from those who make you feel less than others. You deserve to be around people who lift you and who appreciate your neurodivergence as part of your brilliance.

Finally, I want to remind you of something important: You are enough. You are sufficient in your successes, struggles, quiet moments, and loudest victories. You are adequate in your imperfections, your growth, and your healing. You are enough exactly as you are, and that will never change.

Nicci Brochard & Dr. Ben Chuba

With love and gratitude,

Your Past and Future Self

Conclusion

In conclusion, this book celebrates the journey that so many women and BIPOC individuals undertake after a late ADHD or autism diagnosis. It's about embracing neurodivergence as part of your identity and understanding that it does not define you in a limiting way but rather opens up a world of possibilities to thrive. The road to self-understanding and acceptance is not easy, and it's rarely linear, but it is filled with moments of empowerment, growth, and connection.

By navigating the intricacies of adulthood with a neurodivergent brain, we unmask the layers of societal expectation, misdiagnosis, and self-doubt. Through candid stories, practical tools, and cultural insights, this guide provides support, encouragement, and a framework for building a life that truly fits you. It's about challenging the myths, unlearning harmful narratives, and creating a future where your neurodivergence is not something to hide but something to be celebrated.

The journey to healing and thriving is ongoing, but you are not alone. Together, we can break down the barriers that hold us back and create space for neurodivergent women and BIPOC individuals not only to survive but thrive. As you close this book, remember that your neurodivergence is a part of your brilliance, and your future is full of opportunities for growth, authenticity, and joy.

Thank you again from the bottom of our hearts to have put your trust in us (*Nicci and Ben*).